MW00893009

Both Sides of the Canvas

by

Mary Hayden Burgess

authorHOUSE

1663 Liberty Drive, Suite 200
Bloomington, Indiana 47403
(800) 839-8640
www.authorhouse.com

First published by AuthorHouse 11/08/04

ISBN: 1-4184-7574-2 (e)
ISBN: 1-4184-7573-4 (sc)

Library of Congress Control Number: 2004098488

Printed in the United States of America
Bloomington, Indiana

This book is printed on acid-free paper.

Table of Contents

Prelude

November 22, 1942

We were a small group of American Red Cross recruits staying incommunicado at the St. George Hotel in Brooklyn, New York. Late evening we were taken to the docks. We marched smartly up a gangplank, each carrying a handsome black leather pocketbook, a musette bag slung over a shoulder and a suitcase in hand. Our footlockers were to reappear at our destination. And so we set sail—without streamers, without goodbyes—on an unknown ship to an unknown destination for an unknown length of time.

Over was our training in Washington, D.C., mostly lectures at American Red Cross Headquarters. Remarks that I recall:

"All uniformed American soldiers are to be treated equally regardless of race, color, or creed."

"If a man comes at you knee him in the groin. When he bends over in pain grip your hands together and give him a chop on the back of his neck." The worldly girl next to me said in a sly aside, "Just laugh at him and the show is over."

"If you go to a bar take off your uniform." Should we wear a pretty petticoat, in case we actually do go to a bar?

One day an administrator interrupted the class. "I need fifteen volunteers *right now*! Hands went up, some decisively, some half way, and some stayed down. Mine went half up, then down. Let fate take its course and don't push it. The volunteers departed immediately. They spent two and a half years in Iceland.

Most of us signed on as Staff Assistants. This meant we would do any job we were asked to do. We would be serving "able-bodied" soldiers. Other Red Cross workers were specially trained to work in hospitals, to manage ARC clubs, or to be Field Directors and administrators. But *none* were nurses. Nurses joined the various branches of the Armed Forces.

We had physicals and were given shots declared good for anywhere in the world. The FBI vetted us, even questioning my grandparents in Ann Arbor, Michigan. We were issued two grey uniforms and a grey overcoat for cold climates, and two light blue ones for the tropics. Baggage allotment was one footlocker, one carry-on suitcase, and one musette bag, an army issue for incidentals. Our commitment: "Be prepared for the whole war plus six months, anywhere in the world."

We were issued identification cards indicating that in case of capture we ranked as officers—Second Lieutenants, in fact. We were also given metal dog tags attached to metal necklaces, just like military personnel.

Off to war in my summer uniform, which I never wore

My dog tags

I stuffed my footlocker. Indeed, I did pack two pretty petticoats. Also, lots of underwear, and Kotex stashed everywhere; a fine red suit, black heels, a pink angora sweater, and a baggy grey one; a wild dirndl skirt and penny loafers. All for off duty time. Oh, and a satin and net peach evening gown. How ridiculous, but *Be Prepared.*

How did I get here? I had been living at the Dorchester Apartments in Washington, D.C. with my parents. Newly graduated with the University of Michigan's class of 1942, I snagged a temporary job with a lawyer for CBS. I wanted to join the WAVES. No, you would not like the discipline, saith my father. I wanted to join the OSS, the secret service Daddy was in. No, saith my father, there are no Mata Haris these days.

In late August I learned about the American Red Cross. I played hooky from my job and hightailed it to ARC National Headquarters. In two days' time I was startled to discover I had passed all seven interviews, not withstanding that I was only twenty-two, three years under the age limit.

Daddy was away on a secret mission in China. I told Mother my extraordinary news.

She asked me, "Where are you going?"

"I don't know."

"When are you going?"

"I don't know."

"How long will you be gone?"

"I don't know."

A long pause, then she said, "Daddy is in China and your brother Ralston is in the Air Force and you have joined the Red Cross. It looks like I am not contributing much." Shortly thereafter she became a Nurse's Aide at Walter Reed Hospital in Washington.

I had fudged only a little in the Red Cross interviews, when asked if I played an instrument. "Oh yes," said I, "the harmonica." At a music store the variety and sizes of harmonicas dumbfounded me. I purchased the smallest. I took a cab home and started practicing in the cab. The driver stopped his car and turned off the meter. "Miss, may I show you how to play that?" After his artful demonstration I gave it to him and did not make a second effort.

* * *

I have jumped right into an early part of my life, one that would shadow me forever, one that I had tucked away in a far corner of my heart and mind to get on with living. But my friend Val, who chronicles the experiences of WWII prisoners of war, encouraged me to tell my story. It has grown beyond the boundaries of the war into the whole of my life.

First Things First

I was born in 1920, my sister Elizabeth two years earlier, and our brother Ralston four years later.

When Ralston came along, I slipped unwittingly into my appointed slot as "middle child." Elizabeth could always do more as the oldest, and Ralston usurped my place as the family's adored baby. I was not an easy middle child.

More than once Daddy sat on the commode upstairs with me over his knees and the flat of a hairbrush on my bare behind. My biggest fear was that he did not love me any more. How I screamed and tried to get away, but he held me tight until I calmed down so he could tell me how much he loved me. "Just behave yourself so I won't have to bring you upstairs holding on to your ear." Years later he told me that he was so angry that he needed those stairs to gain control of himself. I cannot remember my misdeeds.

I came into the world without a right ear. I was glad to be a girl because I could hide this defect with my hair. In later years I found that it was handy to have enough of a vestige to hook on glasses and wear earrings. There were plusses. It afforded my friends the pleasure of showing off their odd friend. These girls grew up automatically walking on my left side. Another plus has been the ability to sleep on my good ear, never bothered by a barking dog or my college roommate's typewriter or, later, the buzz bombs, the drone of enemy aircraft, the crash of nearby artillery fire.

Ralston thought he too had a defect: flaming red hair. One day our parents were frantic when Ralston did not return from school promptly. They found him at a neighbor's house. He had dunked his head in a can of green enamel paint. He did not want to be called "carrot top." Later he simply didn't reply to anyone who addressed him as Carrot Top or Sonny. He became Ralston, period. It was the same with Elizabeth. She responded to none of the nicknames associated with E. But Daddy had a name for me: Mary, Mary, the Little Fat Fairy. I did not mind because I was not fat. Or was I?

Elizabeth and Mary, The Bay Wall, Manila, 1923

In the mid Twenties we moved to our beloved gray-shingled house at 520 Onondaga Street, home for the next nineteen years.

520 Onondaga Street

In Angell School kindergarten I was enchanted by a boy who had chubby pink cheeks, bright blue eyes and dark curly hair. When we were supposed to skip around the room, skip, skip, skip, I would run to catch up to him. For my effort Miss Robinson made me stand with my face in a corner of the room. By the fourth grade I was over my crush, but even now we keep in touch. He still lives in Ann Arbor.

Riding lessons. A dollar to rent the horse and a dollar for the lesson. Eventually I acquired a horse of my own, a strawberry roan gelding. I rode him throughout high school and college. We did some jumping, even entered small local horseshows. Little did I know how important riding would be in my life.

On Lake Charlevoix in northern Michigan, Kamp Kairphree was a girl's camp for twelve to eighteen-year-olds. I was strictly a camper the first year, but the second year I was a counselor for tennis and horseback riding. I had the nerve to take a group of young girls, none of whom could ride well, to the top of a sand dune and let them slide down almost vertically on their horses! The camp leaders were horrified and, naturally, it was not repeated. But it was fun.

One of my favorite pets was a white rat. I named him Sniffles. At night Sniffles was put in the drawer of the desk between my bed and Elizabeth's. When I got the flu or measles and stayed in bed for days, Sniffles was my great companion on my bed. Daddy chuckled about the time he was passing by our bedroom and I was saying to Elizabeth, "I wish you'd keep your stockings on your side of the room." She retorted, "I wish you'd keep your damn rat on your side of the room!"

When I went off to camp, and Elizabeth was visiting elsewhere, Daddy was in charge of feeding and watering Sniffles. One night he awoke hearing a persistent squeak. Sniffles had to gone to the far side of our parents' bed and gotten on top of a rocking chair to tell Daddy he was hungry. Daddy had forgotten to feed and water him. How did Sniffles know right where he had to go to get fed?

My first watercolor painting, Sniffles

Our dog, Mickey, was of uncertain parentage. He looked like a small setter and was delightful. April 1st of some year, Daddy told me that Mickey had been run over the night before. Not wanting to believe him, I accused him of a bad April Fool's joke. He took me to the garage where Mickey lay. Mickey looked just fine, but dead indeed. I went into great wails of weeping. Daddy said, "Mickey lived a happy life and he was happy when he died. He never knew what hit him. You do not have to feel sorry for him." A philosophy that has sustained me more than once.

Daddy built the white fence for the back yard. Mother grew her flower garden. An apple tree in the front yard was big and motherly. We spent years climbing it. Often Mother would call and call, and I wouldn't answer because I was daydreaming in my favorite perch. How I exasperated Mother! But how closely she watched over me. Truly, I once inspected Mother to see if she had an eye in the back of her head.

Five Twenty Onondaga had a proper back yard for picnics, tenting, plays, birthday parties, and trying to catch robins by putting salt on their tails. In the farthest corner were our swings, trapeze bar and sandbox—farthest away to shake off as much sand as possible before coming into the house. Daddy put up a pulley on the tallest tree. We climbed a ladder and came zinging down putting our feet up to slam against the house. In the corner nearest the kitchen grew a pear tree. The pears weren't very good, but under it were our beautiful white rabbits and bunnies.

An extra bedroom and bath were over the garage. Early in the Depression a family came to our front door and wondered whether we had a place they could stay and whether we had something to eat. They had been in their car traveling for several days, with no place to go and no money. The parents and their children lived in that one room for a few weeks until they could establish themselves.

I asked our parents if we were rich or poor or what. I just wanted to know where we stood in the scheme of things. They said that in the United States we do not have classes. If we did we would be pretty much middle class. People with bigger houses and plenty of help were pretty much middle class also.

Teaching political science at the University of Michigan was not a high paying profession. However, when he took a pay cut during The Depression, Daddy commented on the fact that he would never lose his job. There were always young people to be taught.

The family bathroom upstairs was a good visiting place. I would watch Daddy strop his razor and then, oh so carefully, shave. He polished his shoes, with a spit in the final shine. Mother wrapped herself in a towel and he shaved under her arms for her sleeveless beaded evening gown. The hem was cut just above the knee and the waist was low. She was glamorous even if she was a housewife. In the little sink, Mother washed Daddy's wool socks, wrapped them in towels then hung them to dry—visiting all the while. How else would I have known how to wash my husband's wool socks?

The basement at 520 had a cement floor and cement walls with tiny windows near the ceiling. At the bottom of the steps, Daddy decorated the walls with colorful sleeping mats hand woven by a Moro tribe in the southern Philippines. Upon them was displayed his handsome collection of Igorot and Moro spears. Around the corner was his target and fencing equipment. He practiced there, with much banging. In the winter, he shoveled coal into the furnace.

A little room in the northwest corner of the basement was transformed into Daddy's jewel-like study. An oriental rug covered the cement floor, and the walls were lined with books and mementos. I can still conjure up the marvelous fragrance of his pipe.

There was room for a second chair next to his desk. I often sat there visiting, or being lectured to. Mother sat there proofreading the galleys of the book Daddy was writing. How often Mother stood at the top of those stairs asking him if they could accept this or that invitation. How often the reply was, "No, I have to write." Daddy eventually became chairman of the University of Michigan Political Science department. He had to grab what time he could for his writing. I guess that's the way just about anything gets done.

The book was central to our lives. I refer to it as the bible we grew up with. Even standing at the head of the basement stairs one could hear the tat, tat, tat of his two fingers flying over his Corona typewriter keys as he wrote 984 pages. This definitive work, *The Philippines: A Study in National Development* (Macmillan 1942), began in the early 1920s, after our first trip to the Islands. Besides the book, he was always writing papers on a variety of subjects.

His stints in the Philippines included two as a visiting professor (1922-23 and 1930-31) and one as a correspondent for the Christian Science Monitor (1926). The last was as vice governor general of the Philippines (1933-35), appointed by President Roosevelt despite Daddy's Republican affiliation. Frank Murphy, a staunch Democrat, was the new governor general. He was pleased to have a sidekick who knew so much about the Islands.

In November 1941, Daddy wrote the preface to his book at the Dorchester Apartments in Washington, D.C., just before the attack on Pearl Harbor. How fortuitous, because a whole new chapter in the history of the Philippines began with its invasion and capture by the Japanese.

At the Bentley Historical Library of the University of Michigan there are fifty-six linear feet of shelf space dedicated to Joseph Ralston Hayden's works and correspondence. He had a remarkable life; lucky me to be included.

Mother couldn't carry a tune but was, like my father, a great music lover. Every year the Philadelphia Symphony Orchestra came to Ann Arbor for the May Festival, an event that lasted four days and evenings. Eugene Ormandy conducted his orchestra for Lily Pons, Marian Anderson, Fritz Chrysler, Yehudi Menuhin, Rachmaninov, and other stars of that era. We attended year after year, sitting in the same seats year after year. My eyes often rested on a man three rows down and a little to the left who came year after year. He had a no-ear just like mine.

We had a beautiful rosewood grand piano with ivory keys, handed down through the family. It took up a third of the living room. Both Elizabeth and I took piano lessons in grade and high school. On Sunday evenings, Mother would bring in the teacart and make waffles by the fireside. We would have a little musicale. Uncle Harley played the violin, Elizabeth played the piano, and Daddy, in his beautiful tenor voice, sang. Now I might say: sang songs of yesteryear.

My father explained that had he been an inch taller, he would have gone into grand opera. Then, he teased, he never would have met Mother and there never would have been me. Oh, he would have met someone all right, and gotten married and maybe would have had a little girl. It just wouldn't have been me. How I loved my "inch-too-short" father!

In high school a friend of Mother's read her palm: "You're going to marry a man who is not very tall, has sandy hair and wears glasses." Mother replied indignantly, "No, he's going to be tall and dark." Daddy was not very tall, had sandy hair, and wore glasses. He proposed to Mother on April 6, 1917, the day the United States entered the First World War. They married after he received his commission as a lieutenant in the Navy. Elizabeth, their first child, was born whilst Daddy was on active duty in France.

Daddy's birthplace was Keokuk, Iowa. At Knox College in Galesburg, Illinois, he was a member of Phi Beta Kappa and of Phi Gamma Delta, a social fraternity. He came to the University of Michigan to acquire his PhD. The summer between his freshman and sophomore years in college he sold Wear Ever aluminum pots and pans—what a surprise to find that out. Mother was an Alpha Phi, a social fraternity, at the University of Michigan. She graduated from the university with Ralston in 1950, but her diploma reads "Class of 1917."

Mother and Daddy, August 25, 1917

Mother's brother Richard, our Uncle Dick, was the first American killed in World War One. He was with the American Field Service in Alsace, as was his brother, Uncle Louis. Both were ambulance drivers. Very early on Christmas morning, 1915, Uncle Dick's ambulance was shelled. It was a bitter time for the family, who had just seen him graduate from Dartmouth College. Because of his death, Granny elected to go to Paris to work as a volunteer at The American Hospital.

I asked Daddy whether he'd been wounded during World War One. He said, "Oh, yes. In France I was riding in the sidecar of a motorcycle. We went off the road, and as a result I have a metal plate in my hand."

As it turned out the U.S. Naval Railway Battery No. 4, which my father commanded, fired the last official shot of World War One. These are his written words from November 11, 1918: "There are few days in the history of mankind more momentous than this one. The eleventh month, the eleventh day, the eleventh hour! At ten fifty-eight and half my gun roared for the last time. It landed in No Man's Land some twenty miles away. The shell weighed 1,470 pounds."

Granny and Grandpapa, my mother's parents, were married in her hometown of Grosse Ile, Michigan in the Detroit River, 1885. That afternoon they arrived by horse and carriage at their new home, 1530 Hill Street, in Ann Arbor. They lived there for the rest of their long lives. A farm then, with seventy-five acres, it was built in 1847 and today is in the Washtenaw-Hill Historic District. It was the site of several generations of gatherings, family reunions, weddings, celebrations, births, and deaths.

Grandpapa was a lovely, gentle man. He taught dentistry at the University of Michigan for thirty-nine years.

Grandpapa, Louis Phillips Hall

Elizabeth Douglas Campbell Hall was known as Lily to her friends, but as "Granny" to a multitude of more friends, grandchildren and great-grandchildren. She was petite, strong and joyful. She was instrumental in organizing the Red Cross in Ann Arbor and devoted to work at St. Peters Episcopal Church. Her mother-in-law, Olivia Bigelow Hall, told her to put the silver flatware in the bank, to take it out only on important occasions. But Lily Hall thought otherwise: the silver would be there long after her lifetime and she used it every day. I have some of it and use it every day.

Thanksgiving, Easter, and Christmas dinners were always at my grandparents', with many cousins and aunts and uncles. Christmas Eve was the time to drive by 1530 Hill Street, cornered by Washtenaw Avenue, across from "The Rock," to view its traditional decoration from the year 1916 on: a lighted candle in each window commemorating the birth of Jesus and the death of Uncle Dick.

My ties to tradition were strong, but overseas with the Red Cross I discovered that ties could be broken and yet life would go on.

1530 Hill Street on Christmas Eve

The summer after Uncle Dick was killed, Granny and Grandpapa bought an old 1854 farm seven miles outside of Ann Arbor, just off Huron River Drive. It became known simply as "The Farm." They spent their summers there, with children, grandchildren and great-grandchildren coming and going. Many of us spent our honeymoons there.

Three bedrooms were on the main floor. Up very steep stairs were two double beds, a chamber pot under each. At night we heard the crickets and the frogs. In the daytime we batted mosquitoes. About a hundred paces from the house was the old barn and next to it the outhouse. I'm glad I experienced an outhouse when I was a child, and that it was only in summer.

The Farm in winter

On the nearby Huron River Grandpapa built a small boathouse for a fine canoe. Friends and family alike can recall wonderful canoeing at sunrise, midday and by moonlight, often spotting water lilies and turtles.

The 520 Onondaga house was sold during World War II, whilst Daddy was with MacArthur in the Pacific and Ralston and I were in Europe. Mother returned to her childhood home, 1530 Hill Street, living there until her death at age ninety. By then a young cousin, Paul Favreau, owned and lived on The Farm. He was the very last of our family to be in Ann Arbor. He sold it with apologies to long transplanted relatives.

* * *

Summer, 1924. I met Margery Bursley. We were three years old. We are still Best Friends, now in the twenty first century. Shy and tentative at first, soon we needed a shortcut across Onondaga Street and through a backyard to the Bursley's side porch. Margery is two months older than I; "I'm older than you are so we will play what I want to play." Sometimes she got away with it. Now, in our eighties, I remind her that she is older!

In a journaling class I created a picture journal of my life with Margery. Here are some of the scenes.

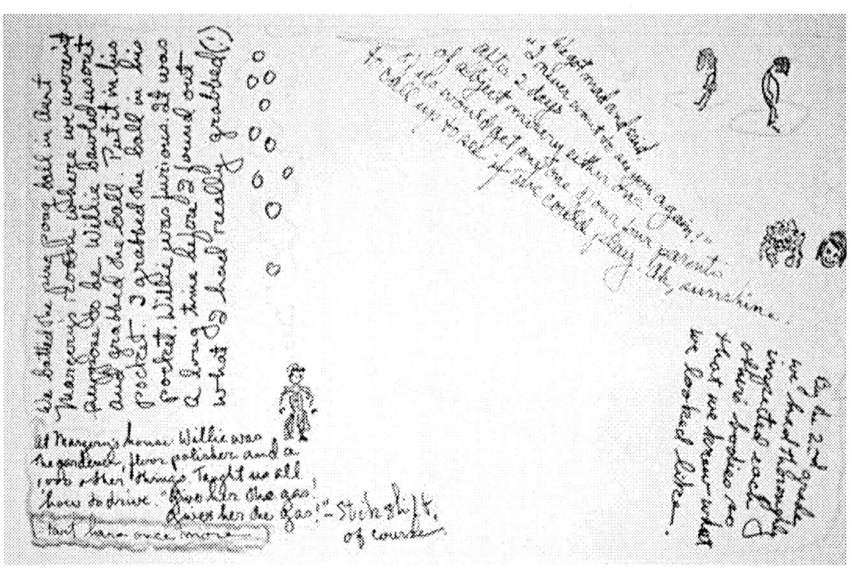

The Secret Eight Club was created in the fourth grade—Aggie Hunt, Connie Lorch, Peggy Whitaker, Marty Piersol, Patty Trosper, Betty Johnson, Margery Bursley and Mary Hayden. Soon we added Bar Brooks and Persie Ehlers. Uncle Joe, Margery's father, inducted us, wearing his collegiate cap and gown. My father, similarly dressed, typed our certificates and added a ribbon. We even got white duck trousers, white shirts, and sailor hats.

Meetings, meetings, meetings, following Robert's Rules of Order as best we could. Picnics, slumber parties, made-up plays and arguments. It was wonderful. Had we continued into high school we might have become a serious society. Our interests changed, but we have kept track of each other through the years, and we are all still living!

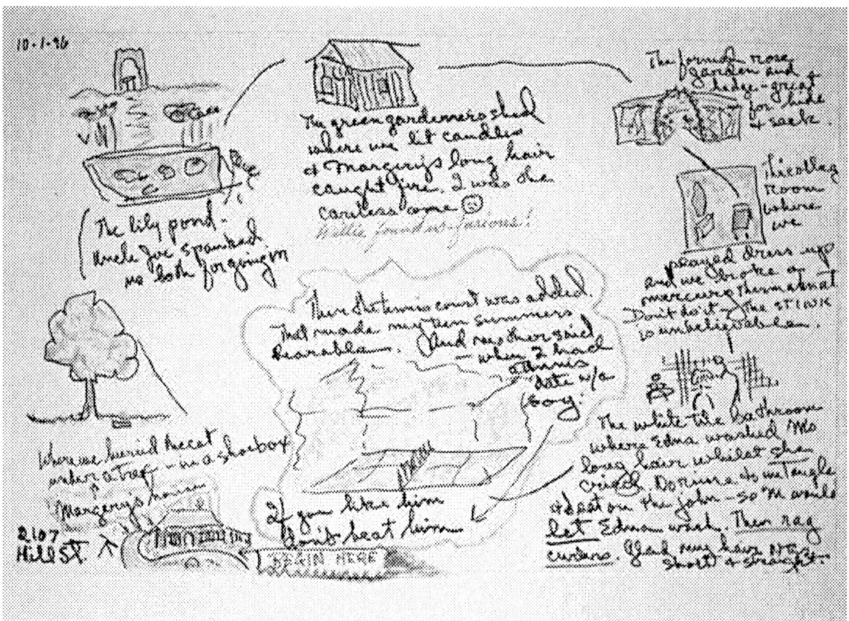
10-1-96
The lily pond.
2107 Hill St.
If you like him
don't beat him
BEGIN HERE

We write letters
Aunt Margery's BLACK
Electric car.
Always had a rose
by the door in a glass vase.
BEGIN HERE
Dandidinmont

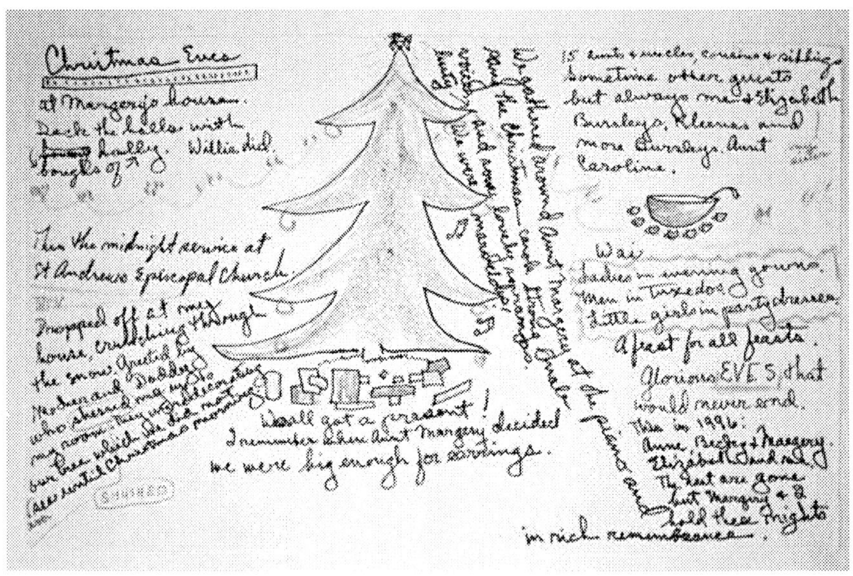

* * *

In 1929, Daddy exchanged our house and a summer teaching job with a counterpart at the University of California in Berkeley. We drove out from Ann Arbor, crossing the country in two weeks. It was very hot. We kept all the windows open. Even on the main road, if we saw a nice little bit of water we would stop and go swimming. We stayed in tourist courts with communal bathrooms, and homes that had a sign "Tourists" offering overnight stays, forerunners of today's Bed and Breakfast.

When we saw magpies Daddy would say, "Well, children, we're in The West!" We heard that six or seven times a day, he was so tickled to be "Out West." When we approached the Rockies, he'd say, "Who's going to be first to see the mountains?" And later, as we approached the island of Corregidor, the entrance to Manila Bay, he'd ask, "Who is going to be first to see Corregidor?" Crossing an ocean: "Who is going to be first to see land?"

It was fun to ferry from Berkeley to San Francisco and Sausalito. We loved looking out through the Golden Gate, never dreaming of a bridge.

In Berkeley I found a store that announced a cream that would "take away freckles." Somehow I managed to acquire it. Very cleverly, I decided to try it out on my freckled little brother. Our parents were most concerned when he showed up the next morning minus a whole layer of skin. I kept quiet and never let on. Oh my, I couldn't do that. He was just a mass of scabs.

Coming home through Yellowstone Park it snowed so hard the windshield wiper couldn't keep up. Daddy could only look out the window to guess where the road was. Who ever heard of snow on September 4?

We stopped to see Old Faithful Geyser. We had waited almost an hour when I said I had to "go." Wouldn't you know that is when the geyser erupted? We had to wait another hour. When I was in college, Daddy gave me a box of crayons with Old Faithful on the cover and chuckled. During the war he sent a postcard of Old Faithful.

In the Park we stayed in two cabins—Mother, Daddy and Ralston in one, Elizabeth and I in the other. Early one morning Daddy woke me up with his hand on the side of my face. He said, "I want you to look up, but don't raise your head." I did look up. A bear had his whole head in the little window above me!

We traveled on to Cody. Elizabeth and I were thrilled to see cowboys on the street. We went to a drug store and bought lipstick for a dime and wore it to the rodeo that evening. Mother told us to wipe it off, and she put the lipstick in her pocket.

Later Mother and I were walking to a garden party in Ann Arbor. In a hurry she reached into her pocket for colorless pomade and smeared it all around her mouth. Only it was our lipstick! The devil was at work in me, saying it served her right for taking our lipstick away in the first place. But my conscience got the better of me, and just before we reached the party I told her. Back home she looked in the mirror and gave a startled laugh. Cleaned up, we returned to the party.

From Cody we took the dirt road over the Big Horn Mountains. With all the curves and switchbacks, one or the other of us got carsick and felt better on the floor in the back. We came down to a beautiful valley of rolling hills and stopped in a little dusty town for the night. We stayed in a fine old inn by the railroad tracks and listened to trains passing in the night. The town and country offered a most romantic setting. It had cowboys too.

* * *

We went to the Chicago World's Fair in 1930. I was intrigued by *Ripley's Believe It Or Not*. It was in a round tent with many little stages, each with its own curtain that opened to show us a "freak": a girl without arms and legs who could draw with her teeth, a man with "crocodile skin," etc. I was intrigued by each and every one and went through the show twice. No one else in the family wanted to see it.

As I was gaping at something, I just knew I heard someone calling my name. I looked up and on one of the little stages stood my father looking over the crowd for me. I waited until he climbed down and then made myself known. I certainly was not going to admit that my father was up on that stage!

The rest of my family was sweltering in the sun waiting for me. I knew then that I had been very selfish. We found the nearest place we could go in and have a cool drink. No chairs, but a slope with nice carpeting. Mother and Daddy were too tired to take us out immediately, even though it turned out to be a striptease act. The ladies wore tassels on their bras which they twirled this way and that. Fascinating!

Those Glorious Philippine Years

As a youngster I had a persistent dream. I was on a large ship. It was pulling away from a dock and a band was playing. Everybody was standing on the shore side of the deck, tossing streamers to those left on the dock. I ran to the far side of the ship, thinking I had to be there to keep the ship from tipping over. A man and a woman found me and were furious for leaving them on the crowded side.

I told my parents about this dream. Perhaps, they said, the dream was a memory from the return trip from the Philippines in 1923. The dock could have been Pier 7 in Manila Bay, or Hong Kong or Shanghai or Kobe or Yokohama or Honolulu, or perhaps even Seattle. Thinking it might be their only chance, our parents had proceeded around the world. A couple, that man and woman, were in charge of getting Elizabeth and me across the Pacific.

The autumn of 1930 found us once more headed for the Far East. Daddy was to teach at the University of the Philippines. We boarded the New York Central train in Ann Arbor, and in Chicago changed to the Southern Pacific for the grand run to Los Angeles. Mother had made navy and white-figured pique dresses, proper traveling dresses complete with hats and gloves, for Elizabeth and me. We were twelve and ten, and Ralston was six.

Mary, Ralston, and Elizabeth in Baguio

How we enjoyed the train! Speeding through the countryside, gazing out the window daydreaming, sitting outside at the very back in the Observation Car, and sweeping grandly into the dining car to select another delectable meal. The dining car had spic-and-span white tablecloths and a bud vase with a rose by the window, sturdy white china, and shiny tableware. The black waiters and porters, in their dark trousers and spic-and-span white jackets, were gracious and thoughtful.

Our parents had lower berths and we three shared two upper berths. It was fun clambering up to our topside beds by little ladders and disappearing behind the dark green curtains.

In Los Angeles, we boarded the *Steamship President Wilson* of the famous Dollar Steamship Line. We made a brief stop in San Francisco, and then sailed out of the Golden Gate, still without a bridge, headed for half way around the world.

Family friends met us at the dock in Honolulu. They took us on a small dusty road to the Royal Hawaiian, a beautiful country hotel. We had lemonade on the veranda by the beach, enjoying the lapping waves of Waikiki.

As we set sail westward into a brilliant sunset, Hawaiian boys dove magnificently off the bridge of our ship to catch the coins that passengers tossed overboard. We had each been given fresh lei and were told that we should toss it into the water to signify that one day we would return. Colorful leis fluttered to the water as Hawaiian guitars strummed "Aloha 'Oe." It was all so wonderful and romantic I had to cry.

The longest haul of the voyage lay ahead: nine days to our next destination, Japan. The Pacific Ocean was mystical to me in fair weather and foul, in blues of every shade, greens, grays, and inky blacks, and often-brilliant hues of warm colors. Sometimes we might have been becalmed had we traveled in the days of sailing ships. The ocean was rich with schools of porpoises and flying fish, and occasional pods of whales. We seldom saw sharks. A ship on the horizon was watched with infinite patience. It grew larger and larger until it finally passed us, only to slowly disappear on the opposite horizon. These were not intimate passings where one might shout, "Yo! Ho!"

Aboard ship, we lazed away the days reading, swimming in the pool, playing deck tennis, shuffleboard, ping-pong, bridge and a betting game with small wooden horses. One could sit in a deck chair in sun or shade. During a storm, we ordered a big baked potato from our deck chairs, and watched the horizon while we ate it so we wouldn't get seasick in the heaving seas. Poor Daddy, flat on his back in his stateroom, just hoping not to heave. Breakfasts, elevenses, lunches, teas, suppers, dinners and midnight snacks kept us well fed. Everyone dressed for dinner then danced to the ship's own band. The band also played when we entered or departed ports of call. Shoes were left outside the stateroom door for a polish before morning.

We frequently peered through the porthole, at the moon, at the horizon, or at the gloom of day. In the evenings we stood on a deck looking for the magic of phosphorescence, and the moon shimmering across the water.

We debarked the *Wilson* in Yokohama, Japan. Eschewing taxis, we clambered into rickshaws for the jaunt to the Hotel New Grand. We took the bullet train to the charming mountain city of Nara. Soft rainy mists and brilliant green rice paddies. Tidy vegetable gardens and picturesque villages. Mount Fuji in the distance.

The immense crowds in Tokyo wore mouth and nose masks. What for? The weather? Or not to catch one another's germs?

We caught the *SS President Pierce* in Kobe and sailed on to Shanghai. Daddy looked up a former student of his, a Chinese scholar, who invited us out for dinner with his wife and many, many children. They were all dressed in exquisite quilted silk robes, except the scholar, who wore black silk. We stepped over two beggars sitting at the entrance of the restaurant.

The meal was elegant, I guess, but to me it was misery. There were twenty-five courses, with sharkskin soup, snake soup, varnished duck, and all sorts of unknowns. We were sitting at a round table with the children, who grinned at us while we smiled back. They were so expectant to know what we thought of each course. We had been told firmly to eat a little bit of everything. Three hours later we were each given a very hot towel to wash our hands and pat our lips.

After we left I told our parents "If ever we're back in Shanghai I'm going to pretend I'm not with you! I will hide on the ship!" But when we did go back a couple of years later I was a little more grown up and happy to dine with them again. I've often wondered what happened to that Chinese scholar during the Cultural Revolution.

Off to Hong Kong, thence across the South China Sea to Manila. Almost a month on the high seas. What a glorious time!

Who was first to spot the island of Corregidor at the entrance to Manila Bay? I don't know. Friends took us to The Manila Hotel. We sat grandly in the wicker chairs on the veranda, sipping lemonade under lazy fans, keeping us blissfully cool in the heat of the tropics.

We lived in the unique Valhalla Hotel in Pasay, just south of Manila. Bungalows on each side of a horseshoe shaped road with a dining room and lounge in the center. We enjoyed our little cottage on its short stilts and its capiz shell shutters instead of windows. There were no screens. We used mosquito nets at night and punk under the table. Bearded Hindus in their native dress with turbans and long black beards stood sentinel behind every two bungalows, guarding against thieves or any other mishap.

We had a houseboy named Santos assigned to us. Among other duties he polished our mahogany floors with wax on the flat side of half a coconut. Barefoot, he skated over the floors until they glowed. His wife Donata was our house girl, and her sister our *lavendera*. It was here that I convalesced from dengue fever.

Directly across Dewey Boulevard was the famous Manila Polo Club, with badminton, tennis, and a swimming pool surrounded by a veranda where we drank half grape juice, half ginger ale and ate peanuts. The *nipa* style main house had a handsome restaurant and bar. The polo grounds had bleachers to watch twice-weekly games. Crack polo horses and riders, mostly US Army and Spanish-Filipino, provided exciting matches. Polo was a popular sport, pre-war Manila.

Air-conditioning was not yet a word. Businesses closed between noon and three. There were two or three sumptuous movie theaters—oh, there we called them "cinemas"—well attended not only for the entertainment but for the cool of the darkened theater. We sat up in the *loge* in comfortable lounge chairs.

We three children were sent to Brent School, a coeducational boarding school in Baguio, one mile above sea level. Because of its tall pines, spectacular mountains, and cool temperatures it is known as "The Pearl of the Orient." It was the summer home to much of the government. Five hours by train from Manila to Dumagete: an open bus on the Zig Zag Trail up, up and up to Baguio and Brent School. The wood school buildings spread out on a beautifully pine covered hill on the very edge of the Baguio. Just before entering the city we passed a sculpture of a lion for the Lion's Club. Then came the Rotary Wheel.

A barrio near Brent School

Ralston's habit was to turn cartwheels wherever he was! Well, some people bite their fingernails. He was put in the toddlers' dorm. Elizabeth and I settled into the girl's dorm, along with other children who came from sugar plantations, gold mines north of Baguio, consulates in Manila, the Army and the Navy, and local areas where their fathers had businesses.

We were one hundred strong, from first grade through senior high. I was in the fifth grade with seven boys and one other girl. I thought that a perfect ratio.

In spite of that I was woefully homesick. I cried myself to sleep on my iron cot with high posters to hold up the mosquito net. Dolly Dimples with her smiling face was on my bed greeting me with comfort.

Brent boys played baseball, basketball and tennis. Boy Scouts were active. Our teams played Chinese, Igorot, Filipino and American teams.

Great school dances, both in the gymnasium and in the *sala* (the living room) of the girls' dorm. The *sala* floor was mahogany, highly polished using coconuts again. There were piano recitals and birthday parties. Chapel every morning in the charming little pine chapel, St. Nicolas. Elizabeth and I were confirmed into the Episcopal Church there by Bishop Mosher.

We took a bus down to Bauang in the Lingayan Gulf of the South China Sea for swimming and a picnic. Inevitably, most of us came home late in the day with terrible sunburns, which we doused with vinegar. Ugh.

Brent school later housed Americans imprisoned by the Japanese during World War II. I chanced to go back there forty years later when it was again a boarding school. By this time the school accepted all nationalities. I walked into the girl's dormitory. The floor of the *sala* was still beautifully polished! The bathrooms and showers exactly the same! Only difference was that the girls' rooms were locked. We didn't have keys.

Brent School, being in the cool of the mountains, starts in September and ends in early June. All other schools in the Islands started in June and ended in early March, avoiding the hottest months of the year.

After the school year we came back to Manila, to the Valhalla, to the Polo Club with its wonderful pool, to the cinemas, to small trips into the countryside to visit great stone cathedrals. They were built by the Spaniards who had ruled the Islands for three hundred years before the Spanish-American War. No wonder the largest population group in the Islands is the Roman Catholic Filipinos. We children complained often about the heat until our parents told us in no uncertain terms that everyone knew it was hot and nothing could be done about it. Don't talk about it!

With Professor H. Otley Beyer we drove to an outlying area to collect Chinese pottery shards, hundreds of years old. I wish I had paid more attention to those treasures.

We rode in dugout canoes up to the famous Pagsanjan Falls. The jungle on both sides of the narrow river emitted strange birdcalls. Monkeys, swinging from tree to tree, screamed at us. The falls are awesome.

No ice cream, no fresh vegetables from the market (farmers and families piddled on them for moisture), but marvelous tropical fruits and avocados. In the provinces, never eat or drink anything that is not boxed or bottled. That meant beer at a tender age. No milk. Never step on the floor without slippers or shoes. Always a mosquito net tucked around the bed. Never mind the cobra skin on the sofa; the snake was just shedding it and is gone.

November 1931: time to go home.

Daddy elected to take the Trans-Siberian railroad from Harbin, Manchuria to Moscow. Mother and we three children boarded the *SS President Garfield* and proceeded to Singapore, Penang, and Ceylon, now called Sri Lanka. I had my eleventh birthday in Singapore. We saw hundreds of monkeys living freely in the Botanical Gardens. We watched the various phases of making rubber, from the tree sapping to the end product. What a strange odor the new rubber had! We took tea at the Raffles Hotel.

On to Penang. Mother hired a car to drive us by tea plantations in the mountains for luncheon. Back in the lowlands we visited the Temple of Snakes. Everywhere! Bright yellow! Free to roam! Only dangerous snakes were caged.

Then the Indian Ocean to Ceylon. We went down the gangplank at Colombo. What seemed like a million people garbed in white were milling around. Again Mother hired a car and driver for a beautiful drive to the mountains. Tea plantations everywhere. On our drive down from Kandi, boys on an elephant, just out of the river, came alongside the car and asked if we would like to go for a ride on the elephant. Ralston and Elizabeth flatly said no. Well, there I was in a dress and there was the elephant without anything on his wet back. I decided that no, I didn't think I could do that. I've always regretted not having hopped on.

We disembarked at Suez. Mother hired an open touring car for the drive across the desert. In Cairo, we stayed at the famous old Shepherd's Hotel, which was later bombed to smithereens. We took tea on the terrace, as did other guests, or perhaps they were having their scotch and soda. About the beds: mosquito netting, yes, but the sheets had a strange rough texture that bothered the tips of my fingers. What do the ads mean by silky smooth "Egyptian cotton?"

Riding camels, we saw the pyramids. In Cairo, we saw the King Tut display. We met our ship, which had journeyed through the Suez Canal, in Alexandria. Sailed across the Mediterranean to Genoa and Naples, then to Marseilles. Train to Paris.

We visited Mother's brother, Uncle Louis, and his French wife and our three first cousins. We stayed in a small pension and had yummy hot chocolate and croissants for breakfast. Ralston and I, both bored waiting for grownups, took great pleasure in filling up the water jugs, opening the windows and pouring the water on the passersby below. Uncle Louis's family joined us at the resort village of Le Portel on the English Channel. A fine sandy beach and gentle waters. We gazed across at the White Cliffs of Dover.

Daddy was still in the frozen north. We caught the *SS George Washington* in Cherbourg and sailed to New York.

* * *

It was good to be truly home again. Good to be back at U. High, with the girls and the boys we had always known.

My first date with a boy: he took me to the movies when we were twelve. My father drove us and his father picked us up. I was furious when the box office lady thought I was thirteen, and Pat had to pay forty cents for me and ten cents for himself. Actually, he had to call his father to come to the theatre with the extra thirty cents. Those three dimes were precious during the Depression. How embarrassing!

In the seventh grade, I met my first secret love. When I saw him, my heart turned over. He was in the ninth grade, tall and dark and handsome. He walked slowly and, I thought, with dignity and perhaps aloofness.

It was like having a crush on a movie star. Unobtainable. That made me feel safe and sure that this paralyzing, numbing feeling—dread, really—would soon go away. But it didn't. Even another two-year sojourn in the Philippines was only a respite. When I returned for the second half of tenth grade, I could hardly believe that exactly the same old feeling for him returned. Pain.

If I saw him walking down the hall, I would quickly hide my glasses—but then I couldn't see the moment he might look at me and say, "Hi." I could hardly walk, let alone talk, and knew my face was grim. I was sure that I was awkward and homely, even without glasses, and had no personality, no redeeming feature.

It helped to have him graduate. It eased the burden just to have him gone—but then I saw him once more at a New Year's Eve party and he casually kissed me on my lips, looked me in the eyes, and smiled, "Happy New Year, Mary." I spoke to no one for two days, nor did I eat. His spell was so great I couldn't leave my room, and my parents thought me ill. A year or two later I realized that somehow the weight of this inexplicable devotion had lifted and I was free, and very happy to have it gone. He never knew.

* * *

In 1933 I had just started the eighth grade in Ann Arbor. I came home for lunch one day and we five were seated at the table. Daddy announced that at eleven forty-five that morning, in the middle of his class, his secretary had come fluttering in with a telegram from President Roosevelt. He had appointed Daddy vice governor general of the Philippines. What a surprise! I was having so much fun with my friends that, true to form, I lay on the floor crying and saying, "I'll be a boarder somewhere. Someone will take me in, so I don't have to go to the Philippines." Mother and Daddy quietly assured me that we would all leave for the Philippines in three weeks time. Mother was wonderful. She took it all in stride.

The girls in the eighth grade were let out of school to bid me a fond farewell at the train station. We all cried.

We boarded the new *SS President Hoover*, its second voyage across the Pacific. The *Hoover*'s third voyage ran aground near Japan. The Japanese bought it for scrap. Oh, my, how much steel and equipment were in that ship.

Because of Daddy's new position we were given elegant staterooms, which I noted with glee. Daddy reminded us children that we were just ordinary Americans despite the pomp and ceremony.

In costume aboard the S.S. President Hoover, December 1933. First prize for Fancy Dress as "Wrigley Spearmint Gum."

Two days out of Honolulu we ran into a typhoon. We were all told we must stay off the decks. Not even the sailors were allowed out on the decks. But I wanted to see what it was like outside in a typhoon, and went out to the railing. As the ship dipped its bow down into the water, even as big as she was, waves washed over the bow and I was swept into the scuppers, the little culvert right next to the railing. I had no chance to purchase a hold. As the ship's bow rose from the water and the stern went down, I slid aft. A sailor happened to be looking out the window and saw me. He ran out, grabbed me by the scruff of my neck, brought me in and shook me like a naughty puppy. He was livid. I'm sure he saved my life.

We landed in Yokohama and made a short trip to the Imperial Hotel in Tokyo. We pressed on and once again had "Dinner in Shanghai" with the learned gentleman and his family. In the beautiful harbor of Hong Kong we drove up Victoria Peak and took *tiffin* (lunch) in friends' elegant, opulent home with a breathtaking view of the harbor. Later, with more friends, tea at the famous Peninsula Hotel.

Once again, "Who would be the first to sight Corregidor?" I don't know. We sailed past it into Manila Bay, docking at Pier 7. A news photographer snapped our picture. On the dock there was much ceremony greeting the new vice governor, including a cadre of American soldiers for Daddy to review.

Officials took us to the Manila Hotel for a cool drink, but, really, the first person to welcome us back was Santos, our houseboy from the Valhalla Hotel. On the spot my parents put him and Donata on the staff with whatever other servants we might have.

Life was glamorous, and I hardly knew The Great Depression was in full force at home. We lived in several beautiful homes for six months each whilst their owners took home leave. When the governor went to the states my father was acting governor general.

In Baguio we lived in Mansion House, the governor's summer residence. Servants came with the houses, including a cook, a houseboy and house girl, a *lavendera*, and a couple of gardeners. At Mansion House there was a major domo with whom Mother reviewed the menu and other household decisions. When alone, I would ring a buzzer and a "boy" would appear. I would ask his name and then dismiss him. I could do that when I was thirteen.

One night when my parents were elsewhere I was the only one for supper. "Miss Mary, dinner is served." The polished mahogany table could seat twenty. I sat at the end, staring at the exquisite bouquet from the cutting garden. With the lights dimmed, the four tall candles gave a glow to the flowers. Two servants stood by. I sat in silence through four courses, so self-conscious I almost choked. I dared not look at the servants, realizing they watched every bite.

Our parents gave a lavish dinner dance at Mansion House for Brent School. An Army band from close by Camp John Hay played the latest hits from the States. Daddy's *aide-de-camp*, Major Garfinkle, was in charge of every little detail. Later, the major survived the infamous Bataan Death March.

We had a picnic away from the Mansion in a spot looking over the mountains. Mother was startled to see that the servants had brought the best tablecloth, the best silverware, and the best dishes for … hot dogs.

The grounds included two tennis courts and a jumping course for horses provided by Camp Hay, with plenty of land to enjoy a long ride. I surely was glad for those dollar lessons I took at home.

Our driver, Maximo, was in charge of our Buick, which we brought from the States. Daddy had his official car and driver with license plate number "4." Our Buick was also "4." That came after the governor's "1," the president of the Senate's "2," and the speaker of the House's "3."

In Manila, Maximo drove me to Escolta Avenue for sheet music. At a busy intersection the traffic cop, resplendent in a white uniform, stopped all traffic and saluted us as we drove through. I saluted him. My parents later told me he was saluting the license plate, not me. At the music store a great crowd gathered to see who would step out. I smiled and waved like a movie star.

In the mountains a schoolmate and I had Maximo drive us to her father's gold mine on a treacherous one car road. I insisted upon driving. Maximo was not happy with Miss Mary. He knelt on the floor in back.

Bishopsted, an exquisite house of Spanish architecture right next to the Episcopal Cathedral in Manila, was home for six months.

One of the houseboys heard me say I would like to have a monkey. He brought me one without a tail. I named her Peko, after a handsome cousin of Margery's. She was on a leash about five feet long attached to a ring around her hips, and attached on the other end to a ring that slid along a horizontal bamboo pole. This pole ran along the veranda four feet from the floor. Our breakfast table stood in the far corner of the veranda, surrounded by tropical foliage and scented flowers. We asked Donata why she went through the house to bring the food. She smiled and said, "Watch." As she walked down the veranda in her uniform and apron with a crisp bow, Peko would sneak up and daintily pluck the end of the bow and run back to the safety of her pole, screaming with delight.

Governor Murphy and his sister Marguerite and her husband Bill came to a dinner dance my parents gave. The *sala* gave on to the veranda. Formal dress was *de rigueur*, and Marguerite's gown was an off the shoulder affair. Guests were dancing to a soft ballad. A sudden shriek: "Mary, mother of Jesus Christ, save me!" Peko had jumped onto Marguerite's shoulder! Smelling salts were given.

Mary and Elizabeth, fourteen and sixteen, on the steps of Bishopsted leading to the bedrooms

Mother, wearing her handsome Mestiza dress

Our last house in Manila was just blocks from the church with a bamboo organ. On my husband Henry's march into Manila after the Los Baños raid in WWII, he and his men took refuge in this church and the soldiers' wounds were treated. Henry had taken some shrapnel in his backside, for which wound he received the Purple Heart.

Back at Brent School in Baguio, we found friends old and new. I adored the Philippines and Brent School after all. Our parents were a day's drive away in Manila.

Mother had met a newly arrived family from the States. He managed a button factory that sewed tiny abalone buttons on tiny embroidered dresses for baby girls. We could even find these dresses in Ann Arbor. Mother admonished us to be nice to their three children at Brent. Why wouldn't we? She wouldn't say why. Well, I don't think they had been around many gentiles. They were the only ones excused from chapel.

The oldest became my roommate. Irma and I seemed to possess the same funny bone. Back in the States we signed our letters "1/2 Ye Hairy Worm." This was a dumb but private name we used for decades.

Mary Hayden = Hary Mayden = Hairy Maiden;
Irma Walowit = Wrma Alowit = Worm.

Thus the two of us were Ye Hairy Worm. Seems to me we spent the whole of eighth grade laughing. In the end Irma was curious to see the Chapel. We were startled to find similarities. For instance we both loved the hymn "Rock Of Ages."

* * *

Balbalasan Journey, 1934

For spring vacation in 1934, I really wanted to go to Manila to play badminton or tennis or, most of all, swim in the pool at the Manila Polo Club and then sit with friends and sip half grape juice-half ginger ale and munch peanuts. But my parents urged Elizabeth and me to take a journey far into the mountains of Northern Luzon, where they had been eleven years before in 1923. Our destination would be Balbalasan, home of an Episcopal mission.

Brent teachers and boys had made the hike a tradition, but this was the first time women were invited. Miss Yeomans, the school nurse, students Patsy Morehouse, Elizabeth, and Mary, joined Bill (a student from Hong Kong), and Masters Griffith and Wood.

Balbalasan is in the country of the Igorots, native mountain people of Northern Luzon not related to the Filipinos. Igorots were traditionally headhunters, but the custom was dying out.

The seven of us boarded the Baguio to Bontoc bus with handwoven Igorot backpacks, our luggage for two weeks. Miss Yeomans also carried bandages and ointments. Our packs were put on the roof, along with chickens, roosters, and pigs. The bus was open sided, and one just hopped on and sat on any wooden bench, already crowded with Igorots.

We arrived at the Bontoc Mission in the beautiful, high mountains carved into by rice terraces. It is said that if all the Philippine terraces were strung together they would circle the world at the Equator. Fed by springs, they are an engineering marvel centuries old.

Rice terraces

We were invited to a *cañao*, a feast and dancing by the fire to honor the gods of rain and sunshine for a good harvest. We were given carabao meat and rice wine. Mr. Griffith told us to eat and drink with a smile. Later the steady beat of drums lulled us to sleep on the floor of the mission porch. Most of the revelers were pretty jolly on their homemade rice wine.

The next morning we set out on another bus bound for Lubuagan. Beyond this town by afternoon we were so bogged down in mud, we spent the next three hours walking, literally knee-deep in mud. I wished I were in Manila swimming and drinking ginger ale with grape juice. That night we slept in a *nipa* schoolhouse up on stilts. We were each given a blanket to wrap ourselves in as we lay on slatted bamboo cots.

The next morning we started our twenty-three mile walk. The foot trail was narrow, mostly single file. *Cargadores*, barefoot and wearing only colorful G-strings, carried our backpacks balanced on each end of a bamboo pole. These three Igorots put themselves into a cadence and it seemed as if they could have walked on forever.

Patsy with a local fellow, who disappeared as soon as the picture was snapped

The trail wound around steep mountainsides. On the inside curve there was usually a spring-fed stream and thick tropical vegetation that completely blocked out the sun. At first we girls would take off our shoes to wade when the streams crossed the path, but that took too much time even though wet shoes would blister our heels. We hiked through rain showers that produced intense rainbows. The air was so soft and warm we dried off quickly. The valleys were green and wondrous, the high hills covered with wild calla lilies and poinsettias, rice, and vegetables.

At a *barrio*, as the small villages are called, the chief invited us to sit on his handsome flagstone patio and drink a little rice wine. Igorots squatted on their haunches. We sat on stones. I noticed many bamboo poles, and looking to the high tops, realized they were each adorned with a human skull. I counted them. Thirty. I glanced over at the chief and he was smiling at me proudly. Weakly, I smiled back. We thanked him and went on our way.

Igorot trophies. The big overhangs to the stilts kept rats from entering the house.

At midday Mr. Griffiths called a halt and asked us to sit down. He gave each of us a Hershey bar for extra energy. Ahead was a swift stream, bounding over boulders to the valley floor way below. The bridge we were to cross consisted of one fat, sturdy bamboo pole. One other pole served as a handrail. With great care, one by one we crossed. Had we fallen we would surely have been dashed to pieces. It was thrilling as well as scary. After crossing that foot bridge, I never bit my fingernails again.

After we crossed the bridge two of our *cargadores* disappeared. They did not want to go into another tribe's territory. Our men had to go after them. Mr. Griffith told us to just continue on the trail. We hiked through rainforests with emerald and sapphire butterflies that were as big as our hands. We sloshed through fallen orchids as through autumn leaves. Towards dusk, Miss Yeomans and Elizabeth stopped by the side of the path. Elizabeth's heels were blistered down to the bone. Miss Yeomans urged Patsy and me to continue.

We entered another jungle in a bend in the path. Sudden and complete darkness enveloped us. We simply sat down in the blackness. After a long silence we began to sing "There's a long, long trail a-winding..." and "Show me the way to go home…" and other ditties. Patsy suddenly said, "Hush, I hear something!"

Well, I didn't hear anything. Patsy said, "Who's there?"

A man's voice said, "It's me."

"Who's me?"

"George. I come from Deaconess Massey. She sent me to greet you." Then he gathered some leaves and put a match to it and used it as a torch. "Put your hand on my shoulder and the next put your hand on hers."

I said, "Patsy, you go first." Thus we walked, aware that we were descending somewhat. "George, how far?"

"Not far. To the river." Utter blackness as the torch sputtered out.

We trudged on. "George, how far to the river?"

"Not far. Almost here." We finally arrived at the river.

"How deep is the river?"

He said, "Not deep. Not deep." So we waded the river until it got waist deep.

"George, how deep?"

"Not deep. Not deep."

When it was up to our armpits, "How deep, George?"

"Not deep." We began to climb out of the river. I'll never forget looking up a hill in the distance and seeing an electric light in a window, the only one in the whole valley. As we came closer to Balbalasan people lit their candles and greeted us with clapping and laughter.

Mother, Father Richardson, and Deacones Massey, eleven years before we made the trip

Deaconess Massey met us at her door wearing her white starched nurse's uniform and white starched nurse's cap. Patsy and I had baths. Heaven! And we donned our one change of clothing. It had taken four months to get Deaconess Massey's bathtub up the single file trail.

Meantime the men had caught up to Elizabeth and Miss Yeomans. They arrived at the mission around eleven p.m. We had hot soup and were sent to bed. Real beds with mosquito nets. The next morning, the Deaconess told us we could go anywhere in the valley in front of the house, but admonished us not to take the trail in back leading to a different tribe's territory. "When our people take that trail, they don't come back."

Morning prayers were at seven a.m., and as in the movie *The African Queen*, with a wheezy old organ in a very native chapel. There was one other white family in Balbalasan: Father Richardson, his wife, their towheaded little boy, and a baby.

Deaconess Massey gave a special dinner party celebrating the fact that eleven white people were gathered in Balbalasan for the first time. This was on her patio. Again, there were bamboo poles surrounding it, but these were topped with torches. She had several boys to wait upon us, complete with white starched jackets. As my eyes slid down, I realized they were still just wearing G-strings and were barefoot. We had an elegant dinner, topped off by finger bowls with a floating orchid.

One morning at prayer, I noticed a little blister on my ring finger. I was wearing a ruby ring signifying my July birthday. By the time the service was over, the blister had grown the full length of my finger. By nightfall, my finger was so swollen that Deaconess Massey summoned a carpenter to file the ring off. He came in and smiled broadly with twinkling eyes, naked except for his G-string. His teeth were filed into points and his gums were bright red from betelnut juice. His tool was a large carpenter's file. When I finally got up my nerve to extend my hand to him, he filed the ring off without touching my flesh.

The next morning I woke up with a similar ailment on my right ring finger, and then on the two middle fingers. Deaconess Massey pierced the blisters and bandaged my fingers.

We were given two native horses to ride. They were very small, but our feet didn't touch the ground. After a short ride, I was again at the Deaconess' clinic, which was located under her house. The horse had shied at something and rammed my ankle into a bamboo fence right at the sharpest point. Another bandage.

Blisters rose on the top of both my thighs and feet. But none of this deterred me from having a wonderful time exploring the country, swimming, and playing Mumblety-Peg with Patsy. Before we left Baguio, both Miss Yeomans and Elizabeth had been disdainful of our bringing along our pocketknives, but we enjoyed our game.

The swimming hole was an exquisite pool, fed by a cool mountain spring and held in by smooth boulders. The local youngsters were diving and jumping and playing "catch me," uninhibited by their nakedness.

Children at the swimming hole

Elizabeth at the swimming hole

Patsy and I shared a room and each had a net to tuck around our beds. One night Pat said, "Oh, its so beautiful here, I'm not going to use my net tonight." I said, "I won't either." In the middle of the night, I heard Pat scrambling for a light. Where her head had lain was a big black hairy spider. We tucked our nets in.

Our three men companions left Balbalasan to trek through uncharted territory to Aparri at the northernmost tip of the island of Luzon. Five more wonderful days and then it was time for us to leave by a different route back to Baguio. Deaconess Massey lent us her own trusted assistant who spoke some English and two other Igorots to carry our backpacks and a pack of food. We carried our own full canteens.

By nightfall we were in a thick pine forest. We stopped along the trail and the men built a lean-to under which we slept. By the fireside Miss Yeomans changed all my bandages. The men looked on with great interest. They wanted to be decorated also. Miss Yeomans showed them two of my sores and said that's why I had to wear bandages. A couple of them promptly picked up twigs, put them in the fire and burned themselves so they could have bandages too. Miss Yeomans flapped her arms saying "No! No!" but she put elaborate bandages on their burns. They were all smiles.

After the night in the lean-to we walked through thick groves of mature bamboo where the sun did not shine. Even without wind they creaked eerily. Two Chinese traders on small Filipino horses came from the opposite direction. The path was so narrow that we tucked in among the bamboo so they could pass.

We were not too concerned by our small water supply, expecting one of the mountain springs to be full. But the streams were dry. The head *cargadore* advised us to take a shortcut straight up the hillside. We struggled straight up the hill to the spring on top. Alas, this too was dry. All of us hot and thirsty, Miss Yeomans poured the last of her canteen water–one half of a cup. We were each to take a sip, including the Igorots, but she peered in and saw a tiny bug. She threw it out. The men were very angry. Deaconess Massey's boy calmed them down.

We learned to put a pebble in our mouth to create more saliva. There was a beautiful sunset but all I could think of was how I wished I were in Manila swimming and having grape juice with ginger ale.

We came to what seemed to be an abandoned *nipa* hut sitting high on bamboo stilts, the first abode we had found since leaving Balbalasan. A campfire was started and a boy went in search of a carabao wallow that might have water. Ugh! Miss Yeomans insisted that it be boiled for twenty minutes. We were so thirsty that we burned our tongues and throats when we finally drank.

One of the men cut a rectangle out of a piece of green bamboo, the ends of which were naturally sealed, filled it half full of rice, put the rectangle back in place and tied it with green grass. Then he roasted it over the fire. The moisture of the green bamboo filled the grains. It was the most delicious rice I have ever eaten.

We climbed up the bamboo ladder and slept on the bamboo-slatted floor. Our *cargadores* slept on the ground beneath. In the morning we were startled to find the hut completely surrounded by carabaos that had come to drink and wallow in the wallow. *Carabaos* do not sweat, therefore the wallows. They also do not like the smell of white men. Presumably this includes white women as well. Our men shooed them away.

Thus began another long day. Having walked across a high divide, we descended quickly. By noon we sat by yet another dry stream. Patsy and I got out our jackknives and scraped the dusty sweat off our arms and legs. We felt rather swell when Miss Yeomans and Elizabeth asked if they could borrow our knives. Still no sign of huts or people.

The country was flat and treeless. The sun smoldered. One large banyan tree standing out on the horizon became our goal. We slumped down under the tree. We straggled further and sat down in a clump of bamboo—very prickly. We opened our last two cans of food, tomatoes, and savored the sweetness and the juice.

Mary and Elizabeth coming into Lagañgilang

We trudged into Lagañgilang Agricultural School. Our mountain *cargadores* said goodbye and were glad to be returning to their highland people. A news photographer greeted us and took several shots. The article in Manila's *Philippines Free Press*:

10 PHILIPPINES FREE PRESS Manila, May 5, 1934.

Vice-Governor's Daughters Brave Mountain Wilderness

Unchaperoned by Men, Sturdy Feminine Quartette Endure Arduous Experience : : : :

By HERMINIO A. FIGUERAS

There is nothing unusual in a company of men going adventuring through mountainous jungles and meeting strange looking people. But when a group of women, foreign and society figures at that, brave the wilderness of the mountain province of Northern Luzon, without a man companion, that is daring intrepidity.

Elizabeth and Mary Hayden, daugh-

Our parents were startled when they opened their paper and read this!

Patsy, Mary, Miss Yeomans, and Elizabeth.
At our feet are our backpacks.

The superintendent had been expecting us. We sat down to dinner with his family. When the meat was served I made the *faux pas* of the whole trip. I asked, "Is this dog?" Our Filipino host just smiled and said, "No, we don't eat dog." But Igorots do.

We slept well on cots…with mosquito nets!

The next morning we were escorted to the Abra River. We stepped onto a bamboo raft, long and narrow. A little woven cover in the middle would seat two. Filipinos poled the raft down the Abra River. A lovely, leisurely trip. As the sun grew hotter, we took turns under the cover, and often slipped off the raft to cool in the water. We passed other traveling and fishing rafts.

Raft on the Abra River

By midafternoon our raft was nudged to an inlet where we got off and clambered up a hill to a road. A bus came along which took us into the coastal town of Vigan. I discovered I could not even put on my sandals, my feet were so swollen with sores and sunburn.

Miss Yeomans scouted around and found the American schoolmaster, who let us spend the night in his house. The next morning we visited a strange building, sort of cone shaped, no windows but the low sides were above ground to let air in. It was cool and dark and silent except for the whirring of pottery wheels. Many Chinese were squatting on their haunches with one foot turning the wheel, fashioning clay water jars. The schoolmaster drove us back to Baguio.

The skin on my thighs, ankles and fingers deadened. The doctor kept cutting it away. A long healing time.

* * * * *

Elizabeth made the same trip the next year. How come? Ah, a certain young schoolmaster was also going, Larry Pearson. He taught Bible and History, and was choir director and baseball coach.

She and three classmates graduated that spring. Shortly thereafter she sailed to France to study at the Sorbonne. She would live with the Picards. Mr. Picard had been carried in Uncle Louis' ambulance during World War I.

In the meantime Ralston and I immediately entered our next grades at The American School in Manila. The school was built of native grasses, bamboo, and wood. The windows had grass overhangs that could be shuttered in heavy rains or typhoons. Because of the heat, our classes started at seven thirty and ended at twelve thirty. At home we rested then made a beeline for the Polo Club pool and also the badminton and tennis courts.

Ralston, Elizabeth, and Mary in the pool of the Manila Polo Club. All swimsuits were wool!

We went to formal dinners at Malacanang, a palace built by the Spaniards about three hundred years earlier. It became the residence of American governors when the United States acquired the Islands after the Spanish-American War. That is where Imelda Marcos later kept her hundreds of pairs of shoes.

Daddy explained that champagne and wine would be offered at the table, and admonished me just to turn my glasses upside down. However, he was at one end of the oval table for forty guests and I was at the other. With a smile I raised my glass to him as I sipped both champagne and wine.

The Carabao Wallow Hunt and Polo Club in Paranaque, south of Manila, stabled U.S. Army horses. Sunday mornings were devoted to riding cross-country, avoiding the carabao wallows. Except once I got dumped right in one. My horse fell on top of me and I was saved from injury because the wallow was watery and its mud was soft. There were three levels of jumps from one pasture to another. These rides were all hell-bent-for-leather. Then luncheons, sometimes horse shows, sometimes polo. Many of us donned tailored riding jackets of Turkish toweling for our heated bodies after the rides. My boots and linen britches and jacket were also made to order by a Chinese tailor.

This is where I met General MacArthur, exactly my height: five feet, six and three quarters inches—shall we say five feet seven?

After one ride, Governor Murphy's brother-in-law suggested we two sneak off to a cockfight. I told Mother he was bringing me home. Okay. A tall structure, made of bamboo, had tiered balconies. We were seated in the fifth. On my left sat a big fat Filipino smoking a big fat cigar. The smoke wafted over me. The betting was high and men shrieked for their favorite cock; poor things. At home in midafternoon, Daddy gave me a casual kiss. And then another one.

He asked, "Have you been smoking?" A dilemma.

"No, I've not been smoking."

"Well then?"

"We went to the cockfights."

My father paced up and down the room, so agitated he could hardly speak. "There is a law against cockfighting! Do you realize how much this would jeopardize the American role in the Islands? How thoughtless of Bill, in his own position as husband of the governor's sister, who is also the governor's official hostess!" Once convinced that we were not recognized he wanted to know all about the fights.

A lawn party by the Bay in front of the Polo Club: exotic table flowers surrounding tiny candled hurricane lamps. The full moon shimmering across the Bay. Punk under the long table to ward off mosquitoes and even less desirable insects. An exquisite dinner served with finger bowls, a flower floating in the water.

On my fourteenth birthday Ann Alger, a Brent friend, spent the night with me at the Vickers house. It was beautiful with polished mahogany floors. Only capiz shell shutters at the windows. Up on sturdy concrete pillars, a stone's throw away from Manila Bay. The tropical sunset across the Bay, beyond Bataan and Marivales Mountain, was breathtaking. In the twilight, hundreds of bats cavorted for mosquitoes.

In the morning, Ralston said Ann and I could borrow his little rubber-skinned kayak. It had wooden struts and two simple seats. Ralston had rigged up a sail on a forward strut. We were still in our pajamas and barefoot when we took it across the grass to the water's edge. We set off figuring out how to use the two double-ended paddles.

It was soon apparent that the tide was taking us out with it. We came very near a large foreign tanker. We looked to land and found the Vickers house almost out of sight. Vigorously we paddled only to watch the little mast of the sail break and fall to the left, still attached to the kayak. Just as I leaned forward to try to break it free a big black snake slithered by. So we just leaned to the right to keep our craft on an even keel. The tide was now in our favor and helped us reach shore. It was late afternoon. We were sunburned and tired and knew we would be greeted with great relief. But nobody had even missed us! Thought we were at the Polo Club next door.

* * *

November 15, 1935.

A most significant date in the history of the Islands. With great ceremony, Manuel L. Quezon was sworn in as the first president of the Commonwealth of the Philippines. The positions of several American officials dissolved, including those of the governor and vice governor.

Time to go home again. After many *despidadas* (farewell parties) Mother, Ralston and I boarded the German *SS Scharnhorst.* Elizabeth had preceded us on the *Scharnhorst's* sister ship, the *Potsdam.*

Friends joined us on deck for a final farewell. Hugs and kisses amidst baskets of tropical flowers and orchid corsages. A steward struck a gong and called, "All ashore that's going ashore!' When our friends returned to the dock we threw paper streamers to them. The ship left her berth, the streamers broke and we were on our way out of Manila Bay, past Corregidor, headed for Singapore. We would sail through the Suez Canal.

Once again, Daddy went to Harbin to catch the train across Siberia to Moscow. He had purchased two pairs of woolen long-johns for the two-week trip, thinking that after a week he would change his underwear. Later he said it was so cold that he did not change and that his underwear stood up by itself when he reached Moscow.

Parts of our trip were bitterly cold, too. I thought about the winter coat that I had left on the bed in Manila. The only coat I had was a white Chinese squirrel-belly coat that Daddy had brought from China. I was very self-conscious in white. Everybody else was in black or brown.

I never felt like such a foreigner as I did on that German ship. The *Scharnhorst* was later sunk during World War II. However, we enjoyed the deck tennis, ping-pong, dress-up parties, costume parties, birthdays, the Captain's dinner, and dancing. I was fifteen and loved to dance. A dark, swarthy young man would come to the table and merely bow, first to Mother and then to me, and hold out his hand. I would dance with him and then he returned me to the table, and with a bow, left. We never spoke a word. When we docked at Port Said, we learned that he had jumped ship, and that he had swindled a large company in Manila, the one our friend Dick Stapler worked for.

Also at Port Said, Mother received a letter from Granny. It included a newspaper article with a picture of Elizabeth, age 17, announcing her engagement to Lawrence W. Pearson. Well, Mother was flummoxed, and it did not help to have Daddy unreachable in Siberia.

I really was not helpful when I said, "Now, Mother, you should know about me, too. I am engaged to Dick." Because I was only in the tenth grade, he had given me a watch instead of a ring. I was disappointed when she did not seem to be particularly perturbed about my engagement.

Our next stops were Genoa and Naples. My recollection of Naples is of a loud, raucous and rather carefree town. Mother took us to see Pompeii. Certain rooms had tiled pictures on the walls depicting a man and woman and I asked, "Mother, what are they doing?" She said, "Never mind, dear," and whisked us out of those little rooms, which I later learned illustrated various positions.

We sailed on to Marseilles, Majorca, and Barcelona. Marseilles was a no-nonsense port, and I watched from the boat as a sailor who had jumped ship was being returned rather forcefully. He was crying loudly. Oh, I felt sorry for him.

Mother, Ralston, and I had a great time in Majorca for three days. It seems to me we did a great deal of giggling. It was the time of my period and I did not have any supplies. Mother went from one bodega to another trying to describe what we needed, and all they would do was find a toilet for her. We finally went back to the hotel and dear Mother cut up her nightie. This was cause for more hilarity, just between Mother and me.

In Barcelona, she bought me a proper winter cloth coat, but it needed a lining, and they assured us that they could get a lining in it by four in the afternoon, as the ship was sailing at five. During the day we went to a museum and a cathedral. Well, we picked up the package at four o'clock, at more cost than expected. It was boxed and tied so that we could be quickly on our way. The coat had no new lining! This was my first lesson in grand deceit. I chose to freeze rather than be self-conscious in white fur. In Madrid we stayed in a lovely hotel with soft violins playing in the background during tea and suppers. What a far cry from loud, piped music we hear overhead today.

I was disappointed not to see any dashing Spaniards. Then, "Look, Mother, there's one." I spied a tall handsome guy. Mother was close enough to hear him speak to his friend...in French. On the train to Paris we hit the Pyrenees in the middle of the night. We were roused and sent outside to present our passports and be identified.

The three of us stayed in a pension in Le Vesinet near the Picards', waiting for Daddy to come down from Moscow. Elizabeth and I would take the train to Paris to see an opera followed by a magnificent ballet. Elizabeth, having been in France for four months, living with a French family and going to a French school, spoke French so fluently that natives did not know she was not native.

When Daddy arrived he wanted to take me to the Folies Bergere, but the Picards were so shocked that he quickly took back his invitation and said, "All right, I'll take all your children and ours to the French circus." Now, that was a pretty voluptuous affair in itself, and there were many jokes obviously on the risqué side. The Picards and Elizabeth laughed uproariously while Daddy, Ralston and I sat mute.

We sailed the Atlantic aboard the *SS Europa*, late December, cold and rainy with high seas. You know where Daddy was. Once more the Statue of Liberty hove into sight. A night's train trip and we were home!

Through all these journeys my constant companion was Dolly Dimples. She had a wonderful smile and was my great confidant. I never allowed her to be in a suitcase. She was in her little green canvas bag, which I carried everywhere just as a woman carries her purse.

Ralston seemed to be visible only at mealtimes. He had permission to go down the hatches to the engine rooms and up the companionway to the bridge. His insatiable curiosity about big ships and little boats eventually led him to a degree in naval architecture.

The old song entitled "Harbor Lights" can still bring up colorful memories of all the harbors at which our ships called. The young divers in Hawaii. In Japan and China coolies would walk up and down special gangplanks into the holds to get loads out and other loads in. Dressed in rags, they were one constant stream of humanity. At the same time large cranes would lift big loads out of our holds and put them ashore. They toiled night and day. Throughout our voyages, we could watch the sailors execute their various chores, inevitably polishing brass or swabbing decks. The ship's officers were to be fallen in love with, dressed as they were in their impeccable tropical whites. The sailors were not to be spoken to, but I could still admire their fine tattoos. It was the only time I ever wanted to be a boy: to be a sailor of the seven seas sporting a tattoo.

The bay at Colombo looked like freckled water, the jellyfish were so numerous and large, and mostly pink.

Growing Up

In the cold wintry days of January 1936, Ralston and I were back at U High, mother back to cooking and housekeeping, and Daddy back to teaching. Back to the snow and ice, to learning the latest songs on the *The Hit Parade*, to Sunday night suppers of waffles by the fire, to Jack Benny and Charlie MacCarthy. Catching up with the lives of old friends, mostly from that tribe of Secret Eighters, who soon tired of sentences that started “When I was at Brent....”

During the following summers I played tennis some part of each day. I found that this exercise was necessary to ease the pangs of adolescence. This could never be explained to anyone, because I hardly knew myself and had no idea that anyone else experienced the same panicky concerns that I did.

Mary Hayden Is Crowned Net Champion

Mary Hayden won the University high school girls' tennis championship at Palmer Field Tuesday afternoon by defeating Betty Fariss in a hard-fought match, 2-6, 6-0; 6-1.

On her way to the final round, Miss Hayden disposed of Sue Keppel in straight sets, 6-2, 6-2. Miss Fariss won her semi-final match from Becky Grafton, 6-4, 4-6; 6-2.

I often rode horseback with Daddy. We were once on the narrow country road near The Farm. I can't remember why I was on a western saddle with that prominent horn. Suddenly startled by something, my mount shied and in a flash was out from under me. I was so apprehensive of the saddle horn, I did nothing to save my fall which was straight down, *kerplunk*, doing a lousy split. I didn't feel hurt at all until I tried to stand. The pain was excruciating. So I lay at the edge of the road and picked at little rocks whilst Daddy took the horses to the barn and returned with the car. Like a sack of potatoes, he put me in the car, then hauled me out at 520 Onondaga. Mother promptly brought out three glasses with wine to sip. Then Potato Sack was taken for x-rays. Nothing was broken, but the ligaments in my inner thighs were torn to shreds. How uncomfortable those weeks on crutches were!

Mary riding with friend Connie Lorch Osler

I took no mathematics after tenth grade geometry. I was happy to be in a high school operetta. I only had one line to sing but I was so self-conscious that I was replaced and was relegated to Properties. One line!

Me to Mother: "How far can I go with a boy?"

Mother: "Nothing below the waist, Dear. Hopefully you save that for the man you marry."

Me to Daddy: "I don't drink now, but when I do, what and how much?"

Daddy: "I cannot tell you what or how much. You will have to discover your own tolerance. But you should always behave like a lady. The important factor in whatever you do is to keep control of it, not let it control you. Almost anything you do is all right as long as you don't hurt yourself or anyone else."

* * *

Summer, 1937

I arrived at the east end of Long Island happily visiting cousins at the summer home of the Salters. Katharine Salter was Daddy's first cousin and her husband Docky was a professor of political science at the University of Wisconsin. Their three daughters and young son were therefore my second cousins. Jean, Pat, and Kate were thirteen, fourteen, and fifteen. Joel was much younger and well beloved. I was the old lady of seventeen.

Cousin Katharine said, "Mary, we have all been invited to Gardiner's Island for a reunion of sorts. Docky doesn't want to go, so neither do I. Joel can stay home, too. Would you please go with the girls and be chaperone?" Hah! Me, at age seventeen? I said, "Sure."

This meant that I could drive the family car to the dock where the motor launch awaited us. We docked at Gardiner's Island, walked up the path that generations of Gardiners had strode before to the high plain where stood the lovely old white manse.

We were greeted warmly by David Gardiner and his house guests, among whom I recall Winston Guest, a suave and elegant Argentinean, a truly beautiful and vivacious woman named Polly, and an older man with glorious blue eyes. So youthful were we that everyone appeared rather old. At least, we knew these to be grownups. Except for a few intimate asides to each other and many giggles, they made us feel at ease.

On this sunny August day we joined them in a walk to the windward side of the island, to sandy cliffs high above the Atlantic Ocean. A man was at the ready to shoot out clay pigeons. Over the cliffs they sailed as we stood entranced by the procedure and the great enthusiasm of the shooters. The Argentinean wanted to clean some oil from his gun and with not so much as a hankie among us, he reached into his pocket and retrieved several ten dollar bills which were duly put to work. We were doubly entranced when he did not want to put the blackened bills back into his pocket and nonchalantly tossed them to the winds. The girls were quick to scamper after them, at which the dark, mustached gentleman roared with laughter.

We were seated at an enormous round table for an absolutely delectable dinner. Memorable was the pheasant casserole the likes of which I have never eaten since. I sat next to the handsome man with the glorious blue eyes. In spite of his rather bulbous red nose he cast an enchanting spell over me by his worldliness, his graciousness, and well, his beguiling charm. For many years I retained an inner glow, and perhaps I still do, when I muse about Blue Eyes with the foreign accent. He was Baron Bror von Blixen, Isak Dinesen's ex-husband.

After dinner, David Gardiner and the Argentinean accompanied us to the mainland in the family motorboat. David and I were in the bow of the launch, but in the twilight and rising moon I kept my eye cast towards the stern. The man from south of the border was close to snuggling Jean when his eye slithered up to mine and he quickly withdrew his hand as he glanced away from my steely countenance. He understood my role and his position, because he came from a land of chaperones. At that moment I felt I had performed the role appointed me.

* * *

Frank Murphy, then the governor of Michigan, came to call on Daddy. He had been governor general of the Philippines when Daddy was vice governor. He had four well-dressed, handsome young men with him. Were they FBI agents? Or guards? I was sent to the grocery store to pick up chocolate ice cream. I have a vivid memory of the governor and these big men, plus three Haydens, sedately eating chocolate ice cream in our modest living room.

* * *

When I was seventeen I longed to join the Rockettes at Radio City Music Hall in New York. I really wanted to be that kind of a dancer. "A chorus girl?" asked my startled parents. It went no further. I would have liked professional ballroom dancing too. Ah, to be like Ginger Rogers with Fred Astaire!

I did not want to go to college but was cajoled into it. Having come home from a second sail around the world, I missed traveling. Now in college, I had a geography class in the autumn. The maples and oaks vied to have the most brilliant leaves. I had such wanderlust that I simply wafted around the campus eschewing all classes, daydreaming.

Surviving my freshman year I repeated, "I don't want to go any farther." I think it was because of French. "So, what will you do with your life?" I became a sophomore.

After that year I begged to be let off the hook. My parents wisely said, "But you are half way through and you will always be sorry if you do not finish what you started." Well, by that time I had really learned how to study and how to answer essay questions. Last two years—not bad at all. My horse was stabled on the edge of town. I rode him twice a week. I was president of the Crop and Saddle Club. We held small horse shows.

Jumping a small ditch

For P.E. I dabbled in fencing, because Daddy was an avid practitioner. Not for me. Figure skating and tennis were fine. I joined Mother's sorority, Alpha Phi, and lived in the Alpha Phi house my senior year. There were always dances, formal and informal. There were dates to The Pretzel Bell, the local bistro where serious beer drinkers gathered. I was roundly teased because I stuck to Coca Cola. I couldn't abide beer and no hard liquor was served in the county. Study hall dates were followed by a five or ten cent Coke. There were many walks to and from anywhere, as students were not allowed to have cars.

A highlight was dinner with President and Mrs. Ruthven and their honored guest, Prince Otto of Hapsburg, pretender to the Austro-Hungarian throne, with me sitting on his right—so that I could hear him!

Millie and I choreographed and taught boys to be a girl chorus line for Mimes, the annual all-male musical. I worked on the *Michigan Daily*. Not my thing. Sorority points were gained by serving on committees, so that's what I did, and even directed an Alpha Phi sing. I decided I would never serve on another committee for the rest of my life. Famous last words.

* * *

Grandpapa developed a "softening of the bones," later known as osteoporosis, and in time became bedridden. The doctor suggested that he should have a couple of tablespoons of whiskey at suppertime. Granny was rather indignant but she acquired a bottle of Old Grand-Dad and placed it next to his other medications.

Late one morning in the middle of an art history class at the University of Michigan, I found myself frantically peeling off the red nail polish I was wearing. I raced to 1530 Hill Street during the noon hour and found that Grandpapa had died within that hour. He did not like red nail polish.

I thought it was strange that Elizabeth and her husband Larry weren't at Grandpapa's funeral. They had come down from Brighton where Larry was teaching. Afterwards Mother said we'd go to the hospital to see them. Their six-month-old second daughter Priscilla had just been diagnosed with spinal meningitis. Elizabeth stopped nursing and sat with Priscilla for two days and two nights in the contagious disease section. The doctors said that even if Priscilla lived, she was already a complete vegetable. Her mind was gone. Elizabeth had forgotten about the state of her breasts and they became as hard as rocks. So she lay on her back for two days with cold packs. Before she died, Priscilla was baptized and then she was cremated by hospital orders. Her memorial service took place on December 23 at St. Andrews Episcopal Church.

Because Priscilla died just three days after Grandpapa's funeral, Elizabeth and Larry wanted only a very small notice in the newspaper. We came home from that service and Elizabeth and I both responded to the front doorbell. There stood one of Granny's oldest friends. Elizabeth invited her in and we sat in the sitting room where Mrs. Bonner presented Elizabeth with the beautiful sweater she had knitted for Priscilla. She did not know that Priscilla had died. I watched in amazement as Elizabeth served her tea and never told her, saying she'd find out soon enough and did not want to embarrass her. Twenty years later, after I lost a child myself, Elizabeth wrote, "You will always have a small child like we'll always have our baby Priscilla."

* * *

The summer after high school I took piano lessons from a young concert pianist who lived on our block. I was so self-conscious and unsure of myself that I simply could not play at the recital. He asked me what I thought I would take in college. Music, maybe? He looked me up and down and said, "Did you ever think of physical education?" I didn't touch the piano for years.

In that same vein, Daddy asked me what I wanted to take in college. Art, maybe? "Oh," he said. "Well. I have not seen you do anything to indicate you could be an artist."

So, when I made up my schedule I had a political science class on the list and also a French class, because a foreign language was required. Daddy looked it over and changed a few things, saying, "You don't want an eight o'clock," etc. When I looked at the schedule again there was no political science. "Because I'm head of the department the teacher might feel awkward about how to grade you."

I never did get the hang of French so I switched to Spanish and ended up majoring in history and minoring in Spanish. Years later, as I rinsed all those diapers in the commode, I often wondered, "What was I doing majoring in history?" Actually, it was a good major, as long as I wasn't going to be a nurse or an engineer or develop a specific skill to earn a living. The experience enriched my life. Besides, I never could have gotten into the American Red Cross Overseas without a degree.

* * *

'Twas the summer of 1941 at Fort Lewis, Washington, near Seattle. I was visiting Ruthie Switzer, the daughter of longtime army friends of my parents, who were spending the summer in Laurelhurst, Seattle. Daddy and the chairman of the political science department at the University of Washington had exchanged jobs and houses for the summer session. I was twenty, in between my junior and senior year at the University of Michigan.

Mary in Seattle, 1941

It was an exciting time and age to be on an army post. Ruthie took happy pains to entertain me with dates with young officers from various regiments. She knew I liked to ride horses, so she arranged a Wednesday afternoon canter with a lieutenant in the 115th Cavalry of the Wyoming National Guard. He was dressed in shiny boots with spurs, riding britches, an army shirt, and that marvelous hat. He stood six feet tall.

Galloping through evergreen forests and over fallen logs was exhilarating. He wore beautiful gloves hand knit by a girl in Ann Arbor. "Oh, was her name Barbara Wheat?" Then I remembered that Barbara and I chatted in the powder room at a law school dance. She said her date was a wonderful law student from Wyoming. "Why, yes!" We had an Ann Arbor connection.

Back at the Switzers, I proclaimed, "If he does not ask me to the Officer's Dance on Saturday night I won't go at all."

"But...but," said Colonel Switzer, "if you don't go that means none of us can go."

"I can't help it," say I, walking on air. Thursday and Friday went by quickly. I went touring with an Artillery Officer.

Saturday morning came and there were anxious looks from all three Switzers when the phone rang and it was for me. Ah, yes, it was indeed Lieutenant Burgess, but only for an afternoon canter. Beautiful day, beautiful ride. Not until we were at the door did he ask me to the dance.

After my second date with Hank, another dance at Fort Lewis, he was just stopping the car in front of the Switzer's when I blurted out, "I think if we got married we'd make a go of it." I don't know which of us was more startled. "Oh," said I, "not now. I don't want to be married now!" Hank looked like he might bolt.

It was a summer romance. To dances I wore white satin with a whirling white chiffon skirt that reached the floor. Hank was resplendent in cavalry twills and boots, with spurs yet! And shiny lieutenant bars on his shoulders. The music was "Jealousy," "My Heart Belongs to Daddy," "Kiss me Once," and always the evening ended with the with "Army Gray", the tune to *Lorelei*. A happy, laughing time.

Henry Burgess, senior picture at Harvard, 1940

Before that summer, in Ann Arbor, I had met a student named Joe. We dated a lot. I even wore his fraternity pin, which at that time meant something pretty serious. He graduated before I did. Knowing my love for the Philippines, he went there to seek his fortune, sure that that was where I would want to live. Meeting Hank made me realize that no matter what, I would not be marrying Joe.

Mary and Joe in Ann Arbor

All the way home to Ann Arbor from Seattle, I composed a letter with great anguish, as I was truly devoted to Joe. On November 11, 1941, Joe called from Manila, an almost unheard of event in those days. He had received my letter, and yes, I confirmed his query, calling off our most unofficial engagement. When he asked if there was anyone else, I don't know why I said there was not, unless I meant that no matter what, I would not be marrying him. It was "if" and "when" I might see Hank again anyway. Joe was very sweet, as always, and told me to give Mother his love and birthday greetings for November 12.

This was, it turned out, a momentous conversation. In late December Joe was captured by the Japs and imprisoned. He remained so until liberated from the Los Baños prison camp on February 23, 1945—by an Army raid behind the Jap lines. Henry, then a major in the 11th Airborne Division, was in charge of the amphibious tractors which carried the starving internees to safety.

* * *

On December 7, the day Pearl Harbor was bombed, Troop E of the 115th Cavalry was on the high seas headed for the Philippines, with Hank aboard.

I had a one o'clock class with Barbara, the knitter of Hank's gloves. We were both concerned for the dashing cowboy from Wyoming. I found a letter waiting for me one noon. Couldn't wait to get to class to tell Barbara the good news—that the convoy had immediately returned to Los Angeles. Barbara hurried in and said, "Guess what! I just got this letter from him and he is all right!" I just let my letter burn in my pocket.

Daddy had joined the OSS in Washington just prior to the war. When I graduated from the University of Michigan, I joined Mother and Daddy there.

By the summer of 1942, the cavalry had been disbanded. Hank was with the Army at Fort Knox, Kentucky, and spent weekends with his brother's family in Bethesda, Maryland. It was the perfect place for another, or should I say continuing, summer romance.

Hank and I sought hiding places—on the roof of our apartment building on 16th Street NW, in Rock Creek Park where there were too many mosquitoes, and in a sleazy hotel downtown, which we promptly rejected. We even drove through the lovely rolling hills of Virginia to Lexington and Vicksburg, where I called Mother to say we were spending the night. Believe it or not, we still resisted that ultimate surrender.

Frank Murphy was a member of the U.S. Supreme Court by then, and we visited him. We sat in the visitors' gallery and observed Frank call a page and give him a card. The page came right to us in the gallery. This note on Supreme Court stationery said, "I think you two should marry." I don't recall the Supreme Court making any other decision that day!

Mary and Henry in Washington, D.C.

It was a Saturday when Daddy left on the train to go to the West Coast to join MacArthur in Australia. Mother was very blue. Ralston had already left for training in Casper, Wyoming, and Daddy was going to stop there to visit him on his way to the coast. Mother was talking to a cousin and good friend, who said to Mother, "Well, Betty, why don't you get on the next train and meet them in Casper?" Mother said, "I don't have money." Cousin did. So Mother threw things in a suitcase and ran down to the train. They had a wonderful reunion in Wyoming. Then Mother went on to San Francisco with Daddy.

In August I joined The American Red Cross for overseas duty. Hank proposed marriage. "Oh, Hank, let's wait until after the war, and then if we are both still alive and in love...." So blithe was I!

Late that summer he flew out of National Airport in Washington, D.C. One could stand on a balcony and wave goodbye, but I couldn't find a dime for admission. I burst into tears, whereupon the guard quickly opened the gate, "Oh, for Heaven's sake, get out there!" I somehow knew this was a crucial farewell for both of us as his plane lifted off into the unknown.

Brief Encounters: Echoes From World War Two

There are many threads to my tale of the American Red Cross during World War II. I could title it:

"Dancing All the Way," or

"Laughing Through My Tears," or

"Bathrooms I Have Known."

But I think I will settle for "Brief Encounters."

At twenty-two, I was one of the youngest. Most were twenty-five or older, and I often felt and was naive. We were all college graduates, but most had had prior jobs. We came from all over the U.S. Our intention was simply to do the best job we knew how at whatever work we were given, although I certainly never expected to be in a boxing ring under spotlights throwing candy and cigarettes to multitudes of soldiers cheering me. Women we may have been, but "girls" we were called.

Our time of service was measured in months, like a baby when you say, "Oh, she's three months old." This was true of soldiers too. I was there for twenty-eight months; other girls were there for thirty or more.

When we went to Holland some Dutchmen asked a couple of our officers, "What do these Red Cross girls do?" The officers explained that the girls serve coffee and doughnuts, serve in hospital units and clubs and in the field; that they are morale builders—but do not do what you might think they do. And the Dutchmen smiled and said, "Oh, we didn't think they were good-looking enough for that."

* * *

Rainbow Corner

My first assignment was in the heart of London, at Rainbow Corner on Shaftsbury Avenue, just off Piccadilly Circus.

Open twenty-four hours a day, Rainbow Corner consisted of two attached three-story buildings with full basements. The first had been an eatery, with a beautiful staircase and dance hall, which the American Red Cross (ARC) converted into a penny arcade, with pennies supplied. The Red Cross does not "take" from a soldier. The cafeteria was upstairs, for which a soldier paid a nominal price, because the British claimed unfair competition if we didn't charge something.

A postcard from Rainbow Corner

The basement held a no-charge snack bar; a small dance floor and a jukebox; and a first aid station, complete with several cots covered with rubber sheeting and with a pail by each. Often, on holidays especially, these pails were filled to overflowing by soldiers who had thought they would drown their sorrows in alcohol. There were inevitably some soldiers who had been mugged, hit over the head, or stabbed–and there were others who were just plain sick and had to go the hospital.

Once I was at the handsome front door when a few soldiers walked in. I greeted a young GI and said, "You know, you don't look very well." With that, he threw up all over my uniform. I took him by the arm and down to the nurse. Then I cleaned myself up.

A nurse was on duty around the clock. There were lovely English nurses, and a male nurse on duty at night, also English. We were very careful never to ask the soldiers any questions about where they were stationed or what their specific duties were. There was one nurse with a foreign accent. I was down there when she was talking to a civilian man; they spoke hurriedly in a foreign language. She was dismissed for being suspected of espionage and trying to get the boys to answer certain questions.

One weekend we had a carnival of sorts. I was assigned to guess the weights of soldiers. I had a partner named Adele Astaire. She was small, birdlike, and vivacious with a wonderful sense of humor. Trying to guess the boys' weight, she would pat them more closely than I would have dared. She was Fred's sister, Lady Cavendish. When she wasn't in her country home she stayed at the Ritz, but she spent a great deal of time at Rainbow Corner as a volunteer.

I often exasperated my boss, Sally, staying too long talking with boys, because I could never resist, even when I should have been off doing something else. Sally and I are still devoted friends in this new century.

Mary and Sally

There was an auditorium with quite a large stage. One evening an enlisted man asked me to go to the auditorium. He sat me down center front and then went to the grand piano on the stage. He played classical music for three hours straight. I was his much-needed audience. In the wee hours of the morning he escorted me home.

The second building of Rainbow Corner had been an elegant club, the Monico. On its second floor was a magnificent high-ceilinged ballroom with crystal chandeliers and tall, narrow windows. This was the room that had been converted into the boxing venue. Dances were held every few nights with marvelous army bands. One was Glenn Miller's. Halfway through the evening it was announced that all lights would be out for twelve minutes. The windows were opened to let the stuffy air out, and the band played on.

Rainbow Corner became my home away from home during that rainy, foggy, gray, cold winter. I'll never forget a day in April when the clouds parted and the sun shone bright and warm. It took my breath away.

Soon after our arrival, several of us decided to dine at the Ritz Hotel. That's when I started smoking regularly. One girl ordered a martini with a lemon twist. The waiter was startled. He hadn't seen a lemon in three years. Going back to our quarters in a cab, the lemon girl shined her flashlight around. Another cabby drove by and said, "Turn off that bloody torch!" Ah, lessons to be learned.

We became accustomed to the total blackout of the British Isles. During all our time overseas, at night we never saw an outside light. Vehicles had tiny slits of red in the rear and white slivers for headlights. The barrage balloons, large gray balloons soaring high over strategic places to avert enemy strafing, hardly seemed out of place.

One evening I was invited out for dinner and dancing. We grabbed a cab and, in the dark, mysteriously arrived at our destination. Going through an elaborate system of screens and curtains that maintained the blackout, we entered a most sophisticated nightclub with candlelit tables, two alternating dance bands and classy people from many nations. The dress was elegant and conservative. I wore my red suit and black heels, and was the only person sporting such a colorful outfit.

London—under her mantle of black and festooned with the barrage balloons, and in spite of great pockets of destruction and poverty, in spite of tucking away the Crown Jewels for the duration—teemed with gaiety. Theaters, cinemas, pubs, dance halls, tearooms, museums, concert halls, and nightclubs thrived, as did the black market.

To avoid conflicting stories from many sources, the nine o'clock BBC evening news was the only broadcast in a twenty-four hour period that reported on the war. Much of Great Britain hushed at this sacred hour to hear the latest developments. Whenever a dance ended, be it an army post, a Red Cross club, or any dance hall in the British Isles, everyone stood at attention to sing "God Save the King" and "The Star Spangled Banner."

The American PX (post exchange) was a remarkable institution in war-torn England. It was open only to American soldiers and personnel, including the American Red Cross. They had such precious things: American cigarettes, silk stockings that the soldiers bought and gave to the British girls or sent home, Planter's peanuts, Hershey Bars (I'm still loyal to them), blue and white striped pajamas and other clothes for American nurses. British soldiers resented American soldiers, in that competition was bitter for girls' attention, and Americans were paid more and had access to items that were otherwise unobtainable.

My first winter in London I was sick, and a British doctor came to see me. Three visiting sailors had just left me oranges, which were sitting on the table. The doctor looked at them longingly. He had seen no fruit for years. I said, "Oh, please take these oranges," which he did. Two months later when I reverted back to whatever ailed me, he came back. I asked him, "How did your family like the oranges?" "Wonderful," he said. "They are still sitting on the mantel."

Many soldiers formed friendships with English families, not necessarily pursuing a daughter, but a welcoming home away from home. My brother Ralston found such a home, and an enduring friendship. Away from home, involved in a very emotional and challenging experience, each of us learned how to cope in our own way.

Attitudes toward our jobs and the soldiers resulted in individual tapestries. But our aim in the Red Cross was always to be ever cheerful and worthy of the job. I cannot say I always lived up to this. I only hoped to keep my feet on the ground. I was twenty-two; too young. However, I kept my nose clean and became known to my friends as a soul searcher.

At Rainbow Corner, if I visited with a soldier for any length of time, I wrote down his name and an identifying feature in a book each night so I could greet him by name if our paths crossed again. Later, when I hit the road in the Clubmobile, hardly a day went by without seeing and greeting some boy who had been to Rainbow Corner.

Each and every day of those twenty-eight months overseas, I learned more about our country, our social customs, our educational system, our vast range of nationalities, including both young immigrants from Europe and Mayflower descendants. I learned a great deal about life and about myself.

One evening, I could see that a certain fervent officer was out to "have me." Walking home from Rainbow Corner—blackout, of course—we struggled a bit. I got away and ran all the way through Berkeley Square. Got my key in the door of my flat across from the Claridge Hotel. I ran up five flights. He caught me before I could open my door. He came in. I exclaimed that I never had, and was not going to start with him. To my relief he simply left.

As American girls, we were okay and inevitably asked, "Where ya' from?" Yes, soldiers identified us with the girl next door, sisters, sweethearts and even mothers. But more than that they wanted us to be their own nationality. An Irish boy thought I was Irish because I had freckles. A young Pole looked at me longingly and finally asked, "Don't you have just one drop of Polish blood?" A long time passed before I realized a group of Jewish boys, who were my buddies, thought I was Jewish also. No, I'm just plain Anglo-Saxon.

A white Red Cross worker in charge of Negro Red Cross units was in the field with no place to have lunch except at the soldiers' mess hall. She sat down to eat with the black GIs, making them very uneasy. Finally one of them smiled and said to her, "For a minute I thought you were white." She only smiled and the boys relaxed.

Clubmobile

After three heady months at Rainbow Corner, I was transferred to Clubmobile and hit the road with coffee and doughnuts. Mr. Gibson, the head of ARC in the European Theater of Operations, called me into his office when he heard how dismayed I was to leave Rainbow Corner. He asked whether I played an instrument. This time I claimed the accordion, and for consolation he made sure I got one. Why do I say these things? It was enormous. I could hardly hang it around my neck.

My first assignment was in Newbury, Berkshire. I was met at the station by my new crew: Diana and Francie. We were together for three months in many situations, and made a good working team. Francie was a big, handsome, good-natured young woman from Old Fort, North Carolina ("neah Asheville"), with a smooth complexion and soft, dark hair that fell to her shoulders. She called me "May-ry." She was thrilled when she saw the accordion, as she loved to sing and played the ukulele. She was unself-conscious, a natural singer—blues, jazz, whatever—and a marvelous jitterbugger. I envied her tremendously. She wore an engagement ring. After the war she went home and married her man, who had been in the service elsewhere.

When I practiced the accordion in my room above a pub where we lived, I was begged to stop. But Francie and I could sing and harmonize together and frequently did so for fun. Then we discovered, to our delight, that we could get the boys to sing with us, or sometimes even take over the entertainment, playing a horn or guitar.

On special assignment in the Clubmobile, Francie and I, with several other girls, were sent to Greenwich and Gurich in Scotland. Troops came in by ship from Italy, North Africa, and America. They came ashore by tender, a ship-to-dock ferry, and then boarded the trains, which transferred them to various places in the British Isles. We served our coffee and doughnuts on the trains. It was November 1943. Misty, cold, and often raining. One frigid, foggy day we were waiting on the dock for the new arrivals to disembark from the tender. They waited also, some eight hundred of them with their helmets, rifles and duffels, looking at the land, while Francie and I paced up and down the cement dock. They asked where we were from. We answered. Then we started to harmonize with songs like "Show Me the Way to Go Home," and asked them to sing back to us. Back and forth we sang "There's a Long, Long Trail," "I've Been Working on the Railroad," and other familiar tunes. Someone brought a microphone, and we all sang. Our feet were freezing. Theirs were too. Once they were in the train cars we went down the aisles with our refreshments and American accents. "Miss Francie, what are you doing here?" Francie turned to find her family's gardener.

Usually plenty of give and take followed, the men asking us where we were from. But after one particular car of Negro soldiers learned my home state was Michigan, they were silent and unresponsive and I was uncomfortable. Later, I realized they were probably unhappy about the racial strikes taking place in Michigan factories. They had identified me with white Michigan. They also undoubtedly wondered why, despite my Red Cross uniform, a white girl was serving Negroes.

Once we boarded a tender that was homeward bound. It was crowded with wounded GIs on litters. Also some "able bodies." A captain learned I was from Michigan. He pursued me as I worked.

"Where in Michigan?"

"Ann Arbor."

"What is your full name?"

I told him. He said, "I will see your Mother on Christmas Day. I will see your father next month in Brisbane, Australia. Here is notepaper. Write a message to each." I did. Received a happy return letter from Mother. Longer to get Daddy's from Brisbane: "Eating lunch with several men, a hand came up in front of me with your handwritten note in his palm. I shed a tear." We were a close-knit family, and the war and long separation made us sentimental.

Looking back, I think I was probably a headache to my bosses. I could produce doughnuts and scrub the Clubmobile as well as anyone, but having a smile and a listening ear for GI talk was my job. I was painfully aware of the bewilderment of many eighteen, nineteen and twenty year olds, and how much they missed their families. If a boy wanted to tell me his woes or heart's desire, I would sit down and listen.

One evening in a "Donut Dugout" in Penzance, Cornwall, some GIs came in after a movie. I turned to one and said, "Pat, why don't you go to the barracks and get to bed? You look so tired." He came and put his arms around me. Tearfully, he softly said, "Not since I left home has anyone ever cared whether I was tired or not." I looked around at the other guys, expecting some joshing remark, but they only stared at us in tender compassion.

I was always dashing off letters to soldiers I met hither and yon. Most of them I knew I would never see again, but I also knew they yearned to hear their names at mail call. Some never heard from their families, or not often enough. Once a soldier asked me to write his worried mother to assure her he was fine and in no immediate danger. Several times I wrote letters for soldiers who didn't know how to read or write. Most would try to hide their illiteracy, but it was wartime and they wanted to keep in touch with family. One man who could neither read nor write was much admired by his buddies and was a great Checkers player. Later, in France, he was promoted to field-grade officer, probably because most everyone else was dead; but, for whatever reason, it was fine because he was so capable. He was killed two days after he received his commission.

I certainly was not an organizer, nor was I even practical at times, although I worked in Clubmobiles where we made doughnuts by the thousands and coffee forty gallons at a time.

Mary and Francie let a soldier mix the doughnut batter. Being a cook, he had clean hands!

On the overnight train to Scotland, I was on my own and going to visit Margery's sister Anne who was a nurse with the Michigan medical unit. We were going to have a little vacation together in Scotland. The train had carriages that would hold six people. My fellow travelers were very reserved. They looked me over very carefully. Two of them were obviously Scottish businessmen, two were Polish officers who spoke no English, and the other was an English civilian. In the early morning we all awoke when the train lurched to a stop. I looked around and burst out laughing. One of the Scotsmen asked, "What is so funny?" I said, "I have never spent the night with five gentlemen."

On another train trip there was just one English civilian in my carriage; portly, well dressed and curious about my job and life as an American girl. He asked if I'd gone to college and I said yes. He said, "Oh, one of those girls." I asked, "What do you mean?" From movies he thought all college girls slept with college boys. I think I got him straightened out. I had a couple of chocolate candy bars from the PX, and I gave them to him. He was touched and said, "I will take these to my children. They have never even seen chocolate."

* * *

Some of us took three days off to visit the sweet city of Bournemouth on the southern coast of England. We stayed in a hotel that was more like a grand home, a vacationing place for all nationalities, including American pilots from a not-too-distant base.

I was walking and talking with a P-38 pilot. We took a path down to the beach below the bluff. We picked our way around barbed wire and stakes—in place to slow down the enemy, we thought. The beach was deserted, and we soon knew why. Everyone on the bluff, including the hotel manager, was yelling at us to come back NOW! We did. Land mines lay buried all along the beach. A bigger warning sign was installed.

Sometimes on Clubmobile runs we found ourselves eating at a GI mess. I remember coming into a hall where dozens of soldiers were already eating at long tables. I became almost paralyzed by self-consciousness, shyness—all those difficult feelings—because hundreds of eyes frankly stared, forks suspended midair, conversations halted, as I walked the length of the hall with a big grin plastered on my face and my stomach in my boots. How many times during those twenty-eight months did I face up to similar ordeals? For those of us who were not naturally extroverted, it was an ongoing challenge.

We were transferred every three months so that we "wouldn't become too attached to any unit or anybody." This meant we lived rather nomadic lives, but we were always falling in love with some unit or some guy. It doesn't take three months. Not only did we move into new territory, but we changed Clubmobiles and Red Cross crews as well.

* * *

One day we happened to go to a Negro unit working at an air base. Of course, it was *all* Negro, and, of course, "Negro" is what they were called. Throughout the war, Negroes and Whites were always segregated. But I had taken to heart the saying, "The Red Cross serves all men wearing the American uniform regardless of race, color or creed." We opened the Clubmobile windows to pass out the coffee and doughnuts, and put a really good swing tune on the Victrola, which blared through our loud speakers. It was my turn to fill the tray with extra goodies, such as cigarettes, LifeSavers, and Copenhagen, and to head out the back entrance to serve the men who had gathered around.

A GI started a fine little dance and I couldn't help joining in—at a discreet distance of four feet. The boys were laughing and clapping and more were gathering around when suddenly a shrill whistle broke through the music and noise. All merriment ceased, the boys stood quickly at attention and were marched off. An enraged white officer came over and told me that such behavior might start a riot!

Didn't I know better? He asked us to leave. When I went to speak to some southern white GIs who had wandered over, I saw true hatred on their faces and they spat on me. We left.

My partners didn't say much about my terrible gaffe. The next day we went back to the same base, but served a completely different group—all white and well away from the previous location. Three flyers came up, looked at me with disapproving frowns, turned and walked away. It was probably the only time during our stay abroad that no one came to the Clubmobile. A call came from London headquarters, discreetly transferring me.

* * *

Midwinter 1943, I was with a crew fortunate to live at Northgate Grange, a charming seventeenth century stone manse in Bury St. Edmunds, East Anglia. We served 8th Air Force Flying Fortress (B-17) and P-47 fighter bases nearby.

Our hostess, in distinctly British tweeds, and her grown daughter welcomed us into their home. What a delight it was to be in a real home! Silver candlesticks and silver flatware. The dining room had been turned into a cozy library, reading and tearoom, heated by a glowing fire place—the only room with heat. "There is a war on, you know." Lovely bedrooms, flagstone corridors and bathrooms. Take a bath and see your breath. But we loved it.

Coming in from flying missions over enemy territory, the crews would pick up their doughnuts and coffee or chocolate and say nary a word to us, nor we to them. But many would return to chat after debriefing. A colonel had flown a mission with a B-17 crew I knew. He kept looking at me as he came through the line, but as usual, didn't say a word. I noticed his face was very red, and I was puzzled that only one or two of the other crewmembers came by. After the debriefing, the Colonel returned and said, "Mary, the rest of the crew is in the hospital because of a fire on the plane. They landed safely but are laid up. They want you to come visit."

I found a Jeep and a driver to take me the few miles to the hospital. The captain was going to recover very well. The navigator had been shot in a "difficult place" and turned away when I came in. Other crewmembers were going to mend. Rows and rows of wounded flyboys filled the ward. Across the aisle was a young man in a cast from neck to toes. Even the whites of his eyes were black. When they started bringing in supper trays, he asked if I would feed him. I did, but this first hospital visit was a shock.

* * *

In Bournemouth a handsome young pilot was wound up like a top. He asked me to sleep with him. I replied that I couldn't do that, but that I was a good listener. Understood. So we went to his room, of regal size with gorgeous wallpaper. He sprawled on one bed and I the other. No smooching. He talked into the wee hours.

His problem: he flew his reconnaissance plane alone. He was afraid his number might be coming up. If he could just sleep with someone he knew he'd do a better job. I told him there were plenty of pretty little English girls around who would be happy to accommodate him. Oh, says he, I never really thought about them. He was married. Then his real problem came out. His lovely wife—he showed me her picture—was French Canadian Catholic. Her family and church had so drummed into her to be a "nice girl" that she was unable to let her husband get too close. To my mind, a true tragedy.

The next afternoon, strolling along the bluff amongst the trees as everyone did, I passed the pilot, and he was grinning from ear to ear. He was walking with a pretty little English girl. He looked back over his shoulder giving me the "OK" sign.

* * *

Another bomber group was served on Thursdays. One fellow made a point of speaking to me. "When we go on a mission, I'm always careful to have something to come back to. Sometimes I leave my bed unmade, some days I know my favorite food will be served. On Thursdays, I know I have to come back to say hello to you."

After serving at another base all day we were invited to stay for dinner in the officers' mess: a pleasant repast. At nine o'clock we had to leave for our billet in Bury St. Edmunds, two and a half miles away. The air was soft, the full moon brilliant. I wanted to walk. A young pilot offered to accompany me, so off we went. He knew the proverbial shortcut on a path through the woods. The moon winked between the branches. Suddenly, I found myself in a tussle, then flat on my back with Young Pilot struggling with my buttons. The trousers of my field uniform had side buttons under a fly which he was having trouble finding. Remembering the side remark during our Washington briefings, I began to laugh…a little desperately. Lying on top of me, he stopped fumbling and asked, "What's so funny?"

"Well," I said, "here we are, two Americans, in England, during a war, fighting in the middle of a path. Dumb."

He immediately stood up, reached a hand to me, and brushed me off. When he offered his arm, I took it. On the steps of our house he said, "I've never had a date when I didn't make the girl."

"So, you've just had a new experience."

"May I kiss you goodnight?"

"Yes." Chaste.

However, my next time at the base I could tell by the way the other pilots looked at me that Young Pilot had not reported a failure.

* * *

Although I wrote Henry my "Dear Amos" letters all during the war, we both dated other people. In fact, while posted at Bury St. Edmunds, I became engaged to a gunner, Richard—suave, worldly, and ultimately a determined suitor. At the movies one evening, he slipped a zircon ring on my third finger, left hand. Too tired to argue,

I let it stay, but without making a true commitment, and certainly with no intention of marrying in the middle of the war. However, evidently we were engaged.

I wrote to Amos. He sent a telegram saying, "Do not marry. Henry." Daddy was in the states and met Richard's parents in Chicago. Lovely people but very reserved.

Soon after I was transferred to Penzance, I received official word that Richard's plane had been shot down over Germany. Parachutes had been seen. That was all. Sometime later I received a postcard from him addressed to "Mrs.," the only way he was allowed to write, saying he was not injured, little else. He was a prisoner of war somewhere in Germany. I did not think I could take his ring off while he was a prisoner.

* * *

Penzance and other towns in Cornwall, as well as in Devon, were home to regiments of the 29th Infantry Division. They had been there a long time, waiting for the big push into France. But how lucky could one be during the wait, flung into the southwest corner of England. The landscape was hauntingly beautiful with its yellow-flowered gorse, gray-green for winter, wild moors and steep cliffs rising in the mist over turbulent seas. Ancient tin mines and potteries dotted the countryside, along with camellias and palm trees.

I came to think of these GIs as mine. The coffee and doughnut day trips were mostly fun since the troops were on maneuvers, not yet in the real war, just biding time. They were always glad to see us.

Two girls on my crew stayed in a private home. No more room there, so I was put up right on the Bay of Penzance at the Queen's Hotel, a rambling four-story affair. Because of wartime restrictions, this traditional Victorian holiday spot was off-limits to civilians. I suspect the manager was reluctant to host a Red Cross girl. *What does she do*? So I was put far away from the lobby, in a corner room on the top floor—a lovely, large, lace-curtained chamber overlooking the bay. On the grounds below, a company of soldiers did calisthenics every day. I loved joshing them from my high perch.

Our Clubmobile was set up by this company's kitchen. While we made doughnuts we welcomed boys not on duty to read, listen to records, or just visit. Most of them were housed in a theater with the seats removed. I was given a rare, quick view of it. Often the GIs wanted us to see where they lived, even though glimpses were strictly *verboten.*

One evening a soldier with a bashed-in look and few teeth walked me back to the hotel after work. He insisted we sit down for a minute on the beach by the Bay of Penzance so he could explain himself. "I must tell you who I am and why walking you home has meant so much to me. Please don't run away. I have been in prison for several years. In fact, they only let me out to join the service." Having shared his burden, he went his way and I went mine, he with his dignity and I with his friendship.

A new Red Cross recruit was assigned to our Clubmobile, and she was very quiet for about a week. Then, after another day of making a couple thousand donuts and forty gallons of coffee and serving them to GIs, she confronted me. Her body stiff and her eyes blazing, she said with great indignation, "I will *not* be called Blondie! And their hands are so dirty!" I smiled and said, "Oh, yes, you'll be called Blondie and learn to love it. And why shouldn't their hands be dirty? We've invaded their work place." And we had, be they foot soldiers, flight crews, mechanics, electricians, carpenters, engineers or coal shovelers.

It took men with every kind of skill to keep an airbase of a couple thousand personnel shipshape. And there were small communities like this dotting the entire English countryside, as well as Wales, Ireland and Scotland—even the remote Hebrides Islands, though only a tiny special army unit there.

* * *

George M. Cohan's song, "For it was Mary, Mary," followed me throughout the war. Glenn Miller's band played it at Rainbow Corner. A band struck it up when I entered an airdrome dance in a hanger outside of London. The boys in a Newbury pub would sing it as I passed through to my room upstairs. Most poignant was a lounge in Heerlen, Holland, filled with 29th Division GIs I hadn't seen since before D-Day, with even the Dutch girls singing it lustily.

* * *

Mario Boni was a colorful thirty-year-old Italian top sergeant, round as a butterball but fit. A positive commander beloved by his troops and by me. A composer of songs, which he sang in a strong tenor with all the pomp of an opera star.

One day Sergeant Boni and his company were on a long march. In the middle of it they halted for coffee and doughnuts, planned by the officers, as always, wherever we served. Sergeant Boni literally commanded me to join them on the march—only seven more miles to go. Many eager grins appeared when I accepted the invitation—or was it a challenge? I was even given a helmet and rifle and ordered to fall in. I managed to match the pace, thrilled to participate in one of the basic maneuvers of all soldiering through the ages and around the world, but not at all sure I'd be thrilled for the whole seven miles.

My Red Cross field uniform, consisting of trousers and an Eisenhower jacket, was blue. At the beginning of the war all U.S. troops had converted from blue denim fatigues to olive drab. A colonel in a Jeep moved slowly down the line. Spotting the blue, he jumped out of the Jeep swearing at the top of his lungs and ordering a halt. "Why is this soldier in blue fatigues?" I was already embarrassed by his language, as were the nearby soldiers. I averted my helmeted head and tried not to look at him. But he insisted. I peered at him from under the helmet. When he realized I was a girl, he was speechless, red-faced, and indignant. Sergeant Boni explained as best he could. The Colonel switched from angry to gracious, insisting I give up my charade and ride back to Penzance in his Jeep. I was vastly relieved.

Sergeant Mario Boni

* * *

For a period of two or three weeks, the men ran night maneuvers on the moors near Penzance. During this time, would we please serve doughnuts and coffee when they finish around two a.m.? Yes, of course we would. My cohorts in the private house simply walked out at one a.m. Well, no such nonsense at the Queen's. The doors were locked at eleven p.m. and opened at seven a.m. I explained that I needed to leave the hotel at one a.m. "No," said the night manager. "No," said the day manager. "No," said the general manager. But there are more ways than one to skin a cat.

The hotel lounge was luxuriously appointed with heavy velvet drapes, thick enough to serve as blackout curtains. Windows reached both high and low, well proportioned for the soaring ceiling and fine view of the bay. The night manager saw no objection to my leaving by window in the dead of night. No rules for that. After a few hours of sleep, I dressed, walked the labyrinthine halls and took the ancient elevator down. In the lobby I nodded to the night manager in his glass cubicle. He nodded back as I headed for the lounge. It was entirely black, like walking into a hole. I parted one curtain enough to raise the window and climbed out. GIs lowered me into their jeep, also with no lights, and away we went. An hour and a half later I returned through the same window. The night manager and I exchanged nods once more as I toddled back to bed. Thus it went through all those night maneuvers. Exhausting, as we had already made and served doughnuts all day.

* * *

I found strength and encouragement in the many letters I received from my family. Both Mother and Daddy kept up a steady correspondence.

Miss Mary R. Hayden	*Dr. J.R. Hayden*
American Red Cross	*A.P.O. 500 – GHQ*
A.P.O. 887	*C/o Postmaster*
C/o Postmaster	*San Francisco,*
New York, New York	*California*
	April 28, 1944

DEAREST LITTLE MARY—

My thoughts are with you and Ralston more than usual these days. You are already a part of the most stupendous and the most terrible exercises of force in the history of the world, and I believe that soon it will be. I can imagine your emotions and the strain which you are under as the hour approaches when the period of final decision is reached and thousands must die or be maimed for life. With your keen appreciation of the feelings of your fellow man, this experience will be a hard one for you. Your emotions will sap your strength and the tension will stretch your nerves.

Keep these facts in mind. "Take it easy" mentally and physically when you can. Keep yourself fit for the important work you are doing. Any American woman would be proud to have your opportunities to serve and comfort our men, to make them feel less far from home and the scenes and people they love. I know of no one better able than you to do these things and I am so proud of the way in which you are doing them that often when I think of you the tears come to my eyes. I feel the same way about Ralston. God bless you both.

The next few weeks will be hard ones for Mother. She will be moving the things out of our house. And at times I am sure it will be a heartbreaking job as well as an arduous one. I can tell you that those who keep the home fires burning often have a harder time than we do who are far from those firesides.

I do not know how long I shall be at the place for which I depart tomorrow or the next day. Hope that I shall proceed with my boss to his ultimate destination. The progress that is being made is heartening, isn't it? The people there are behaving magnificently.

Am looking forward to finding a letter or two from you awaiting at my "long destination." You probably will receive a cable from there before this reaches you. Dear love, little girl, and I'm so glad about your Richard.

— Daddy (handwritten)

Cinemobile

In May of 1944 Francie and I returned to London for training on the Cinemobile, a three-quarter ton Dodge truck, one of the very first with a camper over it, housing a stage that went down one side, a little piano (which neither of us could play), a projector, and a generator. They selected us because of our singing up in Scotland. Other Cinemobile crews were very talented women—singers, pianists, and one who made wonderful sketches of the boys. Francie and I were far down the list in talent, with no experience on a stage. But we had to be prepared to perform some show in case the movies didn't work or equipment broke. We couldn't disappoint the boys. We were to get up and do our little song and dance.

Mary and Francie grounding the Cinemobile's electric generator

This time in London, waiting for the Allied invasion of Europe, was very hard for everyone. We were sent to places near and around London to practice showing movies.

At a house somewhere in London, we were showing movies. Francie ran the projector first and then I showed the movie again for another crowd. At the end, around five p.m., I looked for my partner. Nobody had seen her, so I went into the hall and shouted her name. She hollered back, "I'm here, upstairs. Come quick!" A couple of GIs and I took to the stairs. She was screaming by this time, "In the bathroom!" Then I heard a man say, "Hold still. It won't hurt and I'll be through in a minute." We rushed in to discover a GI suspending her over the tub while another held her around the waist. Smelly liquid poured over her head. Kerosene. Then the boys rinsed her hair under the faucet, shampooed it and let her go. It did the trick. No more lice on her scalp.

* * *

June 6, 1944

D-Day. Francie and I had just ordered hamburgers at the Dorchester Hotel, the restaurant serving meals as an Officer's Mess Hall. When we heard that the invasion was under way, Francie said, "I can't believe the invasion is going on and we're just sitting here eating hamburgers." Neither of us had much appetite.

We stayed in London quite some time waiting our turn to go to the continent. The buzz bombs were becoming a serious problem. These were unmanned bombs, robots. We would hear them come whistling over. When they cut out, everyone knew they were going to glide down and land somewhere else.

One Sunday morning a group of us girls were kibitzing in a glassed-in sunroom. A buzz bomb landed about four blocks away. Suddenly our rooms and the nearby office buildings had no windows.

On June 8 Francie and I went to someone's apartment for the evening. By this time we were used to the buzz bombs, which always stopped by midnight. Ready to return to our quarters at ten, we were puzzled by a new buzz overhead. It cut off. A momentary silence. It did not glide. It came straight down. Boom! Not on us, but we decided to stay where we were overnight, on the floor. These Number Two bombs kept coming over until morning.

From Greene Street, Francie and I were sent to the Dorchester, an elegant old hotel. We had a room on the fourth floor. My brother Ralston, on leave from his B-24 bomber station in North England, came to visit in late June 1944. One night, Francie, Ralston and I were up in the room harmonizing. He had been a choirboy before his voice changed. We heard the bombs. We turned off the lights and opened the windows so we could see them light up the sky and explode when they dropped in some hapless part of London. More and more came and then suddenly cut out. Nervous about where they would drop, we crawled under our beds. But we kept on singing.

Already soldiers were returning to England after the beachhead in Normandy, France, was secured. Several visited us, bringing huge wheels of cheese given to them in gratitude by the French. We ended up with six large wheels. The odor was overpowering. We invited the hotel to take the cheese. In rationed England, the management was pleased.

Finally, in July 1944, we were sent to South Hampton and stayed in simple barracks, with straw mattresses, waiting our turn to board a Liberty ship and cross the English Channel to Normandy. Three girls assigned to each Clubmobile and two per Cinemobile made up the members of our group C. We traveled with the 18th Corps of the 9th Army, attached to Special Services. We also traveled with an artillery battalion.

Waiting on the dock in South Hampton one morning, watching our trucks being lifted aboard by cranes, we saw one truck suddenly stop, swinging from a crane high above the wharf. Looking down the line we saw all operations had paused in mid-air. What had happened? The dockworkers were civilians, and it was time for elevenses—tea.

We boarded the *Scripps*, a Liberty ship, which was supposed to take only one night to cross the Channel. We were actually on board five days, including July 21, my twenty-fourth birthday, while they decided whether to land us on Utah Beach or Omaha Beach, and where they would put us once we landed. Francie and I got out our equipment and started showing movies down in the hold, which was also where we slept.

Eventually, one by one, we were told to disembark. We climbed down a rope ladder onto a landing craft and motored toward shore, accompanied by our Clubmobile or Cinemobile. July 27, 1944, we were put ashore on Omaha Beach and drove up the now famous hill past German pillboxes and war debris.

Red Cross girls disembarking the Scripps, *off of Omaha Beach.*

What a wildly busy place! All sorts of vehicles going in all directions, all sorts of noise, all sorts of people working, and the MPs bawling, "Drive on the right hand side of the road!"

* * * * *

YOSEMITE
GOLDEN WEST
LONE STAR
SOUTHERN BELLE
DIXIE QUEEN
GRAND CANYON
ROCKY MOUNTAIN
RIO GRANDE
LONDON
WINCHESTER
SOUTHAMPTON
BOURNEMOUTH
CHERBOURG
CASTILLY
ST. LO
VIRE
CALAIS
SOMME
SEINE
PARIS
REIMS
VERDUN
VALENCIENNES
BRUSSELS
ST. TROND
MAASTRICHT
LIEGE
AACHEN
ROTTERDAM
MEUSE
WESEL
DUSSELDORF
COLOGNE
RHINE
FRANKFURT
BAD NAUHEIM
WESER
HAMELN
HILDESHEIM
MAGDEBURG
ELBE
LEIPZIG
DRESDEN
BERLIN
CLUBMOBILE
GROUP C
LANDED OMAHA BEACH NORMANDY
JULY 27, 1944
ATTACHED XIX CORPS SSO
LT COL. GEO. S. GOODWIN
COMMANDING
FRANCE BELGIUM
HOLLAND GERMANY
AMERICAN RED CROSS CLUBMOBILE

The Continent

From the end of July until the middle of September 1944, with our tents and trucks camouflaged, we bivouacked in Normandy apple orchards, then in Belgian forests and in Holland. We moved nine times in five weeks, always just a day or two behind the front lines, as close as was deemed prudent.

Lieutenant Colonel George Goodwin from Bastrop, Louisiana, was initially appalled at being assigned to our Group C. He couldn't believe his wartime responsibility was taking care of thirty women. Over time he learned to appreciate his job and ours, and we thought very highly of him. He was soft-spoken and wonderful to us. He said, "Don't go into your foxholes until you hear my whistle." We heard it frequently in Normandy and spent many nights in the ground. After returning to the States, he always sent us Christmas cards, and anyone who mailed him a marriage announcement received as present a beautiful blue Wedgwood pitcher. Henry and I received one as a wedding gift, now with one of our children.

A few soldiers were assigned to our Group C, to put up and take down our tents, camouflage them and our vehicles, dig our foxholes and latrines, and break out our C and K rations. A mechanic to check the six by six army trucks the doughnut girls drove, and of course our little Dodge Cinemobile. I don't know who was assigned to clear the areas of land mines. Emotionally fragile for combat any more, but all right physically, this was a good cadre.

When our men sent up artillery fire we were relegated to foxholes in case any flak came our way. During the days of fighting we didn't move forward or show movies. We would just hang around in our bivouac. I found the waiting very hard. The Army's unofficial slogan, "Hurry up and wait," applies, not surprisingly, to all wars. Sitting on our helmets, although there was a mess table and benches, we ate C rations for days on end. Some of it could be cooked over little burners. We had no milk overseas. Water was stored in Lister Bags, large udders, which hung from each tent.

The Germans would fly over at eleven p.m. every night. We called them "Bed-Check Charlie." They never bombed us. They were after bigger targets. Blackout was absolute. One wouldn't think of lighting a match outside a tent, or even inside. At about the second site in Normandy we were warned, "Go directly from your tent to the latrine or mess tent. Don't deviate. We're not sure all the land mines have been found." We had to navigate in complete darkness. Needless to say we didn't move around at night any more than necessary.

We were traveling in and out of St. Lo after it was taken by the 29th Division. A German post, it had been badly bombed by our people. We had to go through the disfigured and mangled town to show movies to troops on the far side and come back through when we returned to camp. It was beautiful countryside, although we could still smell rotting flesh and see upside down cows, dead and bloated from the impact of the blasts.

Francie and I were sent to a first aid station named *Lemon Aid Station.* A long narrow tent carpeted with wounded men lying on stretchers on stilts four inches off the ground. We had shown movies to them a few days before. A young kid she had jitterbugged with in tall, wet grass called, "Francie!" She replied, "Hey there. When are we gonna dance again?" "Never, I just lost both legs." We kept our smiles on but when we left we wept in horror at the scene.

I wrote a letter to Mother in my tent, my helmet at my feet. I tried to communicate my thoughts, as much as I could. Letters were censored. I didn't want anything cut so I was careful. We could write about anyone, but never say where they came from or where they were going. Mostly we did not know anyway. Command would sample the letters and decide whether to delete anything. If they did, they would cut out sections and stamp the letter "Censored." All of us were given APO numbers so we could receive our mail despite changing locations and without revealing our whereabouts. V-mail letters were reduced in size and then forwarded on.

Near St. Lo, writing to Mother

Cleaning muddy high top shoes in Normandy.
I used my helmet for water.

You could get an education from all ranks. How segregated the officers and soldiers were depended upon the unit. Both felt you should be with them, particularly at the 29th Division infantry base. I dated both enlisted men and officers, a juggling act much of the time. But our Red Cross work was with the enlisted men.

In France we showed movies in barns. Our projector was perched up on the hayloft, the screen across from it. The soldiers sat in the grain to watch. If we set up in a deep ditch, camouflage was put over the equipment and we could show movies to about one hundred soldiers at a time during lulls in the fighting. Although we carried identification indicating we were to be treated like officers if captured, the Army kept us back just far enough to be out of danger. Except once.

Francie and I had been taken to a deep forest, dark enough to show a movie during the day. Betty Grable starred and so did a drugstore. All during the movie, German artillery was going over our heads one way while American artillery sailed by in the other direction. The soldiers were very restless, unhappy to have us so close to the fighting, and told us to go back. Soon after, the colonel who had made the forest-movie-showing decision was transferred.

We traveled through Paris on our way to Belgium. Our convoy headed north through farm country and villages. The inhabitants shook our hands as if we had won the war for them, and gave us little mementos as we passed through, rounds of cheese and gorgeous onions so sweet we could eat them like apples. One lady even held out her baby, insisting I kiss it on both cheeks, even though she, or he, clearly had impetigo. I hesitated, but she was so determined I finally did, and got impetigo myself.

We had been on the road for several hours while traveling in a convoy to northern France. All the girls needed to stop, but there just wasn't any privacy anywhere. Finally, we came to a little hedge. The convoy halted, we got out, and went behind the bushes in a hurry. Two Frenchmen came walking along, talking rapidly to each other, and then, peering over the hedge they laughed and shouted, "*Viva la France! Viva l'Amerique!*" and shook our hands.

By September we were in Belgium. We startled the GIs by arriving only half an hour after their last skirmish with the Germans. We received the familiar warnings: know the password; only walk on the path to the lavatory, as land mines are still a danger. Most of us didn't bother to go down the path at all. After settling into our bivouac, Francie and I showed movies every day while the Clubmobilers made donuts and coffee for the troops. Eventually, three very hungry young German soldiers, who had apparently been hiding out behind the formation of Clubmobiles, turned themselves in to the Red Cross personnel. Smelling the donuts every day was too much.

Francie and I went to "Graves Registration" to show a movie. We were stopped at the entrance and idly visited with the guards for almost an hour. Finally an officer hurried over and invited us into the area. We were confronted by row upon row of canvas body bags. Someone explained why we were kept waiting. They wanted each body or any parts thereof tucked into these sacks so we wouldn't see the dead. American soldiers were digging graves in an orderly fashion nearby. Someone pointed into the distance where other soldiers were also digging. He explained they were German prisoners and they were burying dead German soldiers. "We never let them dig our graves and we don't dig theirs."

I asked to see the list of our GIs. Too many from the 29th Division, from those days at Torquay, Halston, and Penzance. Because I recognized so many, they took the list away. Though my heart was lurching, I left the tent full of smiles. The men in Graves Registration must be among the unsung heroes of any war.

I took a stroll across a grassy knoll, curious about an extremely high wire fence. On the other side, what seemed like hundreds of men were standing, sitting, or lying down. All silent, sober and in uniform. Their eyes followed me, this young woman in some kind of uniform, as I walked down the fence line. A couple of GIs told me to come away. I asked who the men were.

"German prisoners."

"How long have they been here? Do they have food and water?"

Two officers appeared on the scene, and each taking an arm, marched me off. "Don't ask questions and don't talk about them." I never heard any more about them.

One time in France when the convoy stopped, I looked across the road at a high fence and on the fence was the name and number of a unit we had served in Newbury a year and a half before. So I started calling out, "Willie! Whitie! Harry!" They peered over the fence then disappeared as they ran around the end of the wall and came running over. We met with great hugs and laughter.

* * *

Gradually we traveled north through the countryside. In Belgium, or maybe Holland, we were asked to show a movie in an empty barn on the edge of town. The barn walls were lined with rows and rows of shiny disks. We brought in our equipment and put up the screen. Seats were arranged for the men with an aisle up the middle. Half way through the movie an officer interrupted, and told the men to leave immediately to return to the front lines. Dismayed, they followed orders. Their faces showed how hard it was to return to the fighting. We quickly packed our equipment into the Cinemobile and headed out too. Just after we left, the barn took a direct artillery hit, exploding in a tremendous blast high into the sky. All those discs had been land mines! No one was hurt, but the timing gave us chills for days—years.

Although Group C bivouacked together, each crew went out to different army units, led by guides from those units. On one assignment, going up a hill Francie and I lost sight of our guide, Lieutenant Fly. We went faster trying to catch up. We could see a big town ahead of us and thought, "Maybe that's where we're headed." As we rushed along we noticed large cement structures on either side of us. We wondered what they were, but kept on going. Pretty soon Lieutenant Fly came speeding up from behind and stopped us. He was white as a sheet. "Aachen! That's Aachen! We haven't taken that city yet!" He had turned off a long way back to join the tanks waiting to invade the city. Angry and shaken, we followed him back to his unit. The cement structures were called "dragon teeth," jig-jagged structures placed as a blockade to keep American artillery and tanks from coming into Aachen, Germany.

Francie and I had to "go." I whispered to the sergeant, he looked around and whispered to the lieutenant, and he found a captain. By this time a couple hundred soldiers were looking around on our behalf, because they certainly weren't going to take us to their latrine. So, we stood around smiling and making small talk when two GIs showed up with shovels and proceeded to dig a hole on the spot. Someone else brought canvas and set up poles. By now all the soldiers were taking in the situation. When we finally got into our makeshift stall, we looked at each other in disbelief, our faces red as beets. Suddenly a voice said, "Wait a minute, wait a minute," and in reached a hand with toilet paper.

In September we arrived in Holland very close to the front lines. Our quarters were in a school building, with thirty women on cots in one room. It was late in the month and cooling off. After slogging through the mud and sleeping in tents outdoors, most of us caught colds.

We watched Aachen being bombed. We were destroying a beautiful old city because it housed numerous German defenses. It was full of citizens. I crawled onto my cot and lay on my good ear.

* * *

I went with some GIs who wanted me to see a discovery of theirs: a German decoy airdrome. Coming through a forest into a large park, there it was, a large wooden structure already half demolished. A shot rang out. A GI said, "Snipers! Run fast and zigzag!" More shots, but we were not hit.

* * *

In early October, we moved on through a number of little hamlets to Heerlen, Holland, meeting many villagers along the way. We stayed in a very nice three-floor hotel with a lobby, dining room, and basement. I shared a room with just one other girl. Colonel Goodwin said, "Don't get out of bed unless I blow the whistle." I was lucky, because with my one good ear on the pillow, I often was able to sleep undisturged by the German artillery. Other times, we would get up, look at the shelling of the building next door from our window, and be so tired we'd just go back to sleep, even when the buildings on either side of us were on fire. Finally, it got so bad the Colonel did blow the whistle. We hurried to the basement. Our hotel was hit. When we went back upstairs, one girl found a shell had gone right through her closet. Another's bedroll with all her clothes in it was sliced in half. "I haven't a thing to wear!" she wailed.

* * *

From November 1944 through April 1945, Francie and I were stationed at a Precombat Exhaustion Center. Valkenburg, in the province of Limburg, was a charming, small resort town nestled in a beautiful region. The Center, consisting of four or five local hotels taken over by medics from the 9th Army, 18th Corps, was operated as a retreat for soldiers receiving a temporary break from active combat. During December, due to the winter weather, the fighting subsided, but in January came the Battle of the Bulge, though not so-named yet, and the combat escalated. We heard the battle and could see tracer bullets, and the sunporch windows in our hotel rattled. Soldiers came right off the front lines from this battle and other skirmishes, for forty-eight hours of rest and recreation, exhausted and dismayed by the war.

A specific program was followed during their stay, beginning with a special assembly in the same big hall where we showed our movies. A Special Service army band greeted them, as well as the commanding officer who explained the routine. They would bathe, have clean uniforms, stash their carbines and helmets, sleep in real beds, eat three meals a day in a real dining room (no K rations), have a dance one evening, a movie the next, and then be sent back to their units.

Curfew was nine p.m., but until then they were free to walk about town. No looting, and please leave the girls alone. Francie and I were properly introduced—name, state, number of months we'd been part of the ETO, this last a surprising statistic to some of the men. One group of infantrymen had been constantly on the move, practically since D-Day, living in pup tents and foxholes. They hadn't washed or changed clothes for weeks, and were layered with dust and dirt. Standing at the back of the room, Francie and I thought they were black. They were, but were white underneath. After so much time at the front, some soldiers found it difficult to be without their weapons and to sleep above the ground, especially on a second or third floor. Even with the help of sleeping pills, issued to all, often in the morning some would be found under their beds. But at the Center they were temporarily safe.

On their first day, Francie and I would show a movie in the hall, sometimes twice so all could see it. Frequently a USO show followed in the evening. The next afternoon, in another building, the band would play for a dance. The Dutch residents were glad to see us, and the local girls were invited to the dances, but few came. They hadn't danced for the four years of German occupation, and many never had. Because we did dance, Francie and I were in demand. She was the jitterbugger and I liked the waltzes, fox trots, and tangos. During the day and into the night when the soldiers were in hotel lounges, Francie and I made ourselves available to visit. One smaller hotel had a Ping-Pong table that was continually in use. We even had dances in our hotel.

Because of dancing so much, Francie and I had holes in the soles of our shoes. We found a cobbler in Liege who said he could fix them in a week's time. When we returned, the untouched shoes were neatly lined up outside his shop. A man next door came out saying, "I've been waiting for you to show up. After you left, the shoe proprietor was taken away for being a German collaborator." We took our loafers back to the Center, stuffed them with cardboard and newspaper and kept on dancing. Francie's were red, mine brown. When we parted company in April, she gave me a red shoe and I gave her a brown one.

* * *

After the short respite, most of the men had a very hard time going back to the fighting. Our conversations gave us a glimpse of their experiences at the front. Some stories were humorous, others eye opening, but more often they were heart wrenching.

Waltzing with a lieutenant one evening, I saw tears streaming down his face. "I never thought that I would be dancing with an American girl again."

As I was strolling along with some GIs, a loose hen appeared on the sidewalk. One of the boys dashed ahead and caught the chicken, and, just as quickly, pulled back in embarrassment and let it go. "I almost forgot. We're in Holland now, not Germany."

In one of the hotels, during a quick search for a bathroom, a soldier directed me and said he would wait outside. The three stalls were empty, but two GIs came in right away. One said, "This feels so good. I haven't shit in three days." Thinking they would be embarrassed, I waited until after they left before coming out. It was the first and last time I heard that word overseas. Movies and general culture now try to make such words seem acceptable. But I could be with servicemen all day and never hear rough language. Somewhere in England I was sitting down with four soldiers to have tea. Three were very talkative, telling me about their families and hometowns. I asked the fourth one, who wasn't saying anything, about himself. The others laughed. "He doesn't know how to talk without swearing, and he's not going to swear in front of you."

Somewhere on the continent, I remember a man working on his foxhole. He looked up at me and beamed, "Hello, Mary! Gosh it's great to see you again." I drew a blank on this grimy, unshaven individual under his helmet. "Don't you remember me? We met at Rainbow Corner and we went to an Italian restaurant in the Soho for spaghetti. You know, I'm the fireman from Pennsylvania." Now I knew him. He was so sleek and clean in his pressed uniform at Rainbow Corner—was that a year ago?

Sometimes soldiers found their way up to our room. When I answered a knock one evening, a young GI came in. The only place to sit was on the bed, so we sat side by side. I tried to talk, but he said, "No. I just want to sit here with you." We sat in silence, not even touching, for about an hour. Then he said, "Thank you," and left.

Another knock came very late one night. A tall, freckle-faced redhead from a tank outfit was at the door. Very restless, he walked around the room talking about his hometown and his family. Finally he said that his commanding officer had been cut off at the waist and others had been literally demolished. I tried to think of something calming to say or do. "Why don't you sit down and I'll give you a haircut." I put a towel around his neck and cut while he kept on talking. I'd say, "Hold still," or "Just a minute," or "I'll be done soon, don't move." After the haircut we shook hands and he left. The next day the medics who lived next door looked at me askance until I explained exactly what had happened.

Officers seldom came into our building, but one came to my door once and said, "I just want to hug you," which he did. Then he kissed me three times, sweet kisses, and said, "Thank you," and left.

I went out with a colonel, a doctor, who was stationed nearby. The head medic of the center said to me, "Oh please, be nice to him. We get all our supplies through him, all our sheets, all our medicines, everything." I couldn't believe it depended on me and I still am not sure. Would he have withheld much needed supplies if I had refused a date?

* * *

Francie and I shared a bedroom at the end of a hall on the second floor. The medical staff, enlisted men who helped with medical needs, and the American Red Cross Field Director occupied the other rooms in that area. He was in charge of entertainment and counseling soldiers, helping them with crises at home. Our room had two sinks, and the WC for the whole floor was right next to our room. The bathtub, long and luxurious, was at the opposite end of another hall.

One day, after a bath, I emerged with my head wrapped in a towel, wearing a sturdy long-sleeved white seersucker robe with a big, deep red floral print. The dentist's "office" was just across from the tub room, and he snared me saying, "You come in right now and we're going to clean your teeth. I never can nab you, but here you are." Seven a.m., wet hair, in a bathrobe, and I was having my teeth cleaned. His dental equipment looked like a treadle sewing machine—he worked the drill with his foot—but we got the job done

* * *

On my way out the front door of our hotel in Valkenburg a soldier called, "Oh! Mary!" As I said "Yes?" I took a step forward, and down I went into an open manhole, landing on three soldiers fixing the hotel's plumbing.

* * *

Once Francie and I went with some American soldiers in a Jeep to pick up some German prisoners. We were actually in Germany for the first time. The prisoners turned out to be old men and young boys. These were the last resort of the German army. We all got on the Jeep, ten or eleven of us, and our GIs took them to a house commandeered by Americans. These soldiers were from Texas and had started their lives with the German language, and were therefore put to work as interpreters. The prisoners were put up against the wall with hands up, and they were patted down. Their wallets were produced, and we were shown pictures of sweethearts and family members. Francie and I felt this too personal and were very embarrassed.

* * *

I never quite got used to being told at the dinner table, or during breakfast, about a buddy whose brains were blown out, or his guts spilled, or his arm or leg suddenly gone. I would listen intently, then slip up to our room and cry.

On Christmas day we were taken to a hospital filled with wounded American soldiers and were asked to visit with them. The rooms were lined with cots. I moved down one side of the aisle; Francie went along the other. I approached one patient who was getting plasma. A boy in the next cot said, "I think he's gone." We called the nurse and she said matter-of-factly, "Well, he doesn't need plasma anymore." When we finally left the ward, we cried once more.

* * *

In Valkenburg, I received a letter from Mother saying my brother, Ralston, had been shot down, but was all right. He was a top turret gunner and engineer on a B-24 Liberator. Coming home from a mission over Germany his plane, full of holes, was forced to crash into the North Sea. A British rescue boat picked up the survivors in the Channel. Ralston, positioned in the top turret of the plane, was knocked unconscious. As the plane was sinking, he was revived by the cold North Sea long enough to open the turret and dive into the water. Another crewmember's hand was stuck—his neck was cut and his hand was inside his neck, he being too cold and shocked to know. He survived to fly another day. Only one man was lost. The British rescuers gave them a shot of rum, wrapped them in warm blankets and they were returned to their base. No flying for awhile.

Ralston

I really wanted to see my brother. I wrote Red Cross headquarters, but too many people wanted to return to England to see some wounded man or relative. All requests were being turned down. About that time an infantry colonel visited. He said, "I have a seventy-two hour pass to England. Starting at the top, they're sending us back for R&R." I asked how and when he was going, and whether he thought I could sneak on the plane. He didn't know, but later his bodyguard and driver picked me up and took me to the air base in Belgium.

The plane was delayed. We had lunch—generals, colonels, and me. I confided that I was AWOL, trying to get to see my brother. When it was finally time to board the plane, the lieutenant in charge of the passenger list was checking off each person's name. My friend said, "Oh, er, she's the Red Cross worker assigned to the plane." So he let me on. I heard another colonel talking roughly to a private, ordering him to get the luggage on board. I was surprised by his rudeness. Later I realized he was actually helping the young man get back to see his new English bride, by hiding amongst the luggage.

When we landed at Heathrow, which was strictly controlled by the British, an officer was checking everyone off the plane. I fled to the upstairs lady's room. Of course, by now, all the officers on the plane knew about me. Finally, someone knocked on the door and said, "Mary, everyone is waiting for you. The bus for London is outside." I went to face the officer in charge, admitting I had no leave papers. He didn't look happy, but the generals and colonels standing behind me frowned, willing him to let me through. He did, grudgingly. Wonderful!

Eventually, via both train and car, and despite a midwinter blizzard, I arrived at Ralston's base in northern England. He was surprised and pleased to see me. I met his crew. About twenty thousand men were at the base. An officer came over and said, "Why, Mary Hayden." He had lived across the street from us in Ann Arbor. Because of the crowd, he and Ralston had never even run into each other until then.

After the visit, I found my way back to London, mostly by train and bus this time, to comply with the end of the seventy-two hour leave. It was so foggy—total pea soup—that nothing was flying.

For three days and nights we played (including the colonels and generals). We had dinner and went to a different club every night. I carefully avoided Red Cross headquarters, fearing I would be recognized. I wore the wildly flowered dirndl skirt with the pink sweater that didn't match and had a marvelous time, a real respite from life on the Continent. When I finally returned to Belgium and then Valkenburg, without incident, I asked Francie whether I'd been missed. She had told folks I was off visiting "the troops."

The following week I was sent specific orders to visit my brother in England, orders I couldn't refuse, so I went again, this time by boat to southern England and then by train to the north.

* * *

Home at Last

From my time in Valkenburg one particular dance stands out in my mind. A young officer cut in. It was Dave with whom I'd grown up. His unit had seen severe, intense fighting. He said, "Mary, go home. You just don't belong here." Inside I knew he was right. I couldn't do it any longer. I stayed until an order came in early April. Headquarters requested I take a thirty-day leave in the States. I frankly explained to headquarters that I no longer had the stamina to return. I was in London for three weeks. They didn't know what else to do, so finally let me go.

Before leaving for London on my way home in April 1945, I was sent to a central place in Paris where people got information and permission and travel orders. There were lots of service people around. Across this big expanse I noticed a soldier was looking at me, and began hopping on one foot and the other and then tapped on the shoulder of his companion whose back was toward me. The companion turned around and it was Ralston! His crewmate had recognized me. I let out a holler and called him by name and we ran across the floor and gave each other a big hug. Immediately, we were surrounded by his crew and by many others. And I said, "This is my little brother! This is my little brother!" And he said, "Don't call me *little* brother."

An American soldier had given me a German pistol, a Luger, as a souvenir. I didn't know quite what to do with it. Ralston and I had supper. Afterward we went up to my room and I asked him if he wanted to have it. He looked at it for a long time and then said, "No, I don't think I want this gun. Someday I hope to marry and have children and they'll ask me how I got this gun and I'll have to admit, 'Oh, your Aunt Mary gave it to me.'"

Easter of 1945, I was aboard the *Queen Mary*, going home. All portholes were locked and painted black, the whole ship being blacked out, as we zigged and zagged across the Atlantic. There were thousands of wounded below deck. We girls spent mornings and afternoons with them, carrying magazines, cigarettes, LifeSavers, and smiles.

Easter services were held throughout the ship. I attended one in the small chapel and sat next to a tall young officer. He was a fine tenor and I was thrilled to sing the familiar Easter hymns in harmony with him. We both stared straight ahead. After the final "Hallelujah" we turned towards each other smiling. I said, "I felt I was singing with Daddy," and he replied, "I envisioned being next to my wife." I never saw him again. My last brief encounter.

Coming into the harbor past the Statue of Liberty, I fully expected to be in tears. Oh, boy, here I am coming back to American soil. But I didn't cry then or when we docked. Many did have tears in their eyes. I thought, I've just gotten to be hard-hearted and tough. In the big customs building we were greeted by Red Cross women in uniform. One of them offered me a big glass of milk. My tears overwhelmed me. I took an overnight sleeper to Ann Arbor where Mother and others greeted me at the station. And then I really cried, loud and clear. Mother said, "Do you really have something wrong with you?" "No," I said, "it's just because I'm home."

* * *

One brief encounter had long lasting repercussions. It followed me home. A medic in Holland decided I had scabies, probably picked up in a bed in Valkenburg, recently occupied by a German, despite clean sheets. Scabies are minute and thrive and multiply under the skin—typically wrists, thighs, and ankles, but not above the neck. The prescribed calamine lotion didn't help at all, and I itched constantly. I hoped the German, whoever he was, itched as much as I did. On the ship going home, sixteen of us shared a stateroom. My wrists were noted and I was firmly designated as last in line to use the toilet, sink and shower.

Back in Ann Arbor I went to see Dr. Wile, head of the dermatology department at the University of Michigan. He gave me a warm welcoming hug, but when he learned the reason for my visit, excused himself and returned in his white coat and rubber gloves. Aha, think I, too late! He prescribed a heavy mustard-colored salve with a pungent odor. I was told, "It will stain anything you touch, but put it all over your body, except your neck and head. It smothers scabies."

At Granny's I donned a favorite prewar wrapper. Mother and I made up a bed with old sheets and covered a chair so I could sit down. If some salve rubbed off, I put on more. Even my meals came up to me. I smelled and looked too awful to appear downstairs.

After three days and three nights the scabies were gone. Or are tiny carcasses still under my skin?

* * *

It was good that I came home from Europe when I did. One morning I was with Mother when a telegram came that read, "I'll be on the two fifteen train this afternoon. Joe." Was it Daddy or Joe Hart? We weren't sure. Mother fixed up her room in case it was Daddy, and I tidied up the guest room in case Joe Hart arrived. Mother didn't think it was going to be Daddy, because he hadn't included 'Love' in the message, but Daddy was the one who got off the train. He had left the Philippines in a rush and traveled in such a hurry, he couldn't even stop before he took the train out of

Chicago. He never liked to arrive at his final destination on a plane because he was apt to be airsick. He'd finally been able to send a quick telegram from Kalamazoo, two hours from Ann Arbor. He was a distinct yellow, due to the atabrin everyone took to ward off malaria.

Mary, Joe, and Betty Hayden, Ann Arbor, 1945

Several days later, he and I went to Washington D.C. He gave his report to the State Department. I gave mine to the Red Cross. Daddy and I met every evening for supper. We had three years of experiences to share. We inevitably stayed at the dinner table until the lights were turned off. About the third night Daddy chuckled and, nodding toward the waiters, said, "I wonder what they are thinking about us." Having that week with Daddy was one of the greatest gifts in my life. He had been with MacArthur, had gone back into Manila with him, and had been on secret missions to China traveling over the Himalayas. We were *simpatico*, as always.

At the end of the week Daddy wanted to stay in Washington over Saturday night to attend the wedding of General Parker's daughter. I elected to go home Friday. When he took me to Union Station, he gave me a Moro silver filigree ring from Mindanao. I arrived in Ann Arbor the next morning, and Ralston had just made it home from England.

Ralston had had his last bombing mission earlier that week and one crewmember, his roommate, was on another plane to make his last mission so that he could return home with his crew. He had had a cold so he could not go one time and had to make it up. Sadly, that Liberator went down. He was killed. So Ralston's last duty in England was to was pack up his roommate's belongings to be returned to his family.

Ralston had a wonderful, long talk with Daddy on the telephone. That evening Daddy went to the wedding and reception at the Army and Navy Club in Washington. When he was served champagne, he said, "You know, I feel as if I've already had a glass or two. I'll just go back to the University Club." A motorist noticed him staggering along the sidewalk. When he realized Daddy was ill he helped him into the back of his car. By this time Daddy couldn't talk. With a sad smile he reached in his pocket and handed the man the invitation to the wedding and reception. The man dashed into a drug store and called the Army and Navy Club. General Parker told him to take Daddy to Walter Reed Hospital immediately.

At four a.m. on Sunday the phone rang. The hospital said Daddy was gravely ill. When mother called back, she was told he had arrived at eleven p.m. and died five minutes later, May 19, 1945. The final diagnosis was a cerebral hemorrhage. Daddy had suffered from high blood pressure for years. His family had a history of it and of strokes. That's why he had been a civilian working in the State Department and not in uniform.

Strange as it might seem, we felt quite triumphant that he made it home. And he had often spoken of hoping to go as a whole person. It was a great comfort to all of us that he had. We learned later that after his physical at Walter Reed the Thursday before his death, he'd been told to go home and lead a very relaxing life, and not to rejoin MacArthur's staff, or to return to the Philippines, as had been requested by the Philippine president. Daddy was fifty-seven years old and Mother was forty-nine. I often wonder if I should have stayed in Washington with Daddy. But, no, it was more important that I be with Mother.

When I called Frank Murphy, the friend of Daddy's who had been governor general of the Philippines and then governor of Michigan and was now on the Supreme Court, the morning after Daddy died, he immediately said, "You're an impostor. This can't be. I was with him last night." After verification, some officials went to The University Club to retrieve Daddy's secret papers. He had been given his last paycheck the day before. It had not yet been endorsed. It took Mother three years to get it cashed.

Mother granted an autopsy request, hoping it would further medical knowledge. He was put in the sitting room, where Grandpapa had been. Callers who didn't want to visit the sitting room could use the parlor. I put on an old sky blue sweater Daddy had given me in college and never left his side for two days and two nights. Mother understood, never suggesting I go elsewhere. He was cremated as Grandpapa had been.

Joseph Ralston Hayden

I knew Mother's life was the one that would change, and mine would go along whatever course it was going to take, but it took me a long time to figure out how to live without Daddy. Because he had been gone so much during the war, Mother found herself, in the months after his death, sitting down to write him a letter. She understood that death is as inevitable as birth and life itself. She lived with great dignity forty-one more years.

During my senior year in college I had dated a friend of Ralston's whose service was the Naval Air Force. His name was Bob Sundquist, nicknamed Sunny. He was flying in formation somewhere over the Pacific when they went through a cloud. In that short time he disappeared. A great search took place but neither he nor his plane were ever found. Back in college Ralston dated Sunny's sister Mary Jane. They married in 1947.

* * *

During this same period, my engagement to Richard ended. He came to Ann Arbor and really pushed his suit, saying I was all he thought about during his imprisonment, and he fully expected us to marry. We even put an announcement in the paper with his picture, and I visited his elegant, caring parents in Chicago. I felt his mother and I could be good friends, even though she was very aloof during the visit. Back in Ann Arbor, I asked others what it was like to really be in love. Did they have a heavy feeling of dread before marriage? While Mother was ironing, she and Richard held a long conversation, which ended in a verbal struggle. He finally admitted he was adopted. This seemed to be a devastating revelation for a man who often spoke of how much he was like his father. It also finally came out that he already had a wife! No wonder his parents had been so reserved.

I took Richard to the railway station for his return trip to Chicago. He had his foot on the train step when I firmly put the zircon ring in his hand. He flung it over my head into a grassy bank as the train moved out. I looked at that small hillside a long time, and then walked away. Richard threatened to come back and kill Mother, and maybe me. I called his mother to ask if we were really in danger. She reassured me that he was not a strong enough person to carry out his threat. I never saw him again.

Mother and I talked with our minister. I told him, "I just want to marry someone like Daddy." He replied, "There is no one exactly like your father, but he could be someone with the same ideals."

* * *

That summer after the war ended, friends and relatives trickled home from overseas. We spent time laughing and singing. I don't remember any of us talking much about the war. I had frequent headaches. I was emotionally drained. As I became busy with other things, I was finally able to tuck a little more away. Later, when I would bring it out again to give a talk, I would be transported right back to the war years. Afterwards I would go home, do laundry or the ironing (of course the ironing), mumbling to myself and reliving the whole war over again, until it could finally be released and float away once more. My children asked and always wanted to know more. I could say a little, but not much. I rarely brought up the topic in casual conversation. I don't think any of us did. If I had started to talk, I wouldn't have been able to stop, like the character in *The Rhyme of the Ancient Mariner*.

Love And Marriage

After Daddy's death, trying to recover from the war, I took the train to visit Francie and her husband in San Antonio, Texas. I was hoping to hear from Henry when he returned from Japan. For something to do I took a job as a salesclerk in Joslyn's. I was quite a failure. I was reminded that I was supposed to stand up all eight hours, "and don't lean against a wall." I was put in the Better Dress Department. I approached a couple of ladies and asked if I could help them and an old sales clerk fiercely said, "Don't you cut in on my customers." After that I carefully watched. Later a woman came in with her two daughters. They tried on all the dresses, and dropped them all on the floor. I've never dropped a dress on the floor since then, and didn't before, but this experience made me even more mindful. A middle-aged woman had been watching me. She finally came up and we spoke. No, she wasn't interested in clothes, but she wondered if I'd like to work down at the serviceman's club. I said, "Oh, I might like to do that." She looked at me and said, "You are Jewish, aren't you?" I said, "No." She said, "Oh, never mind then."

After the BDD I clerked in a liquor store. I assured mother that it was prohibited to open liquor in the store. Mother answered cheerfully, "I'm coming to visit you and we'll take a trip to Mexico." She was sure she did not like my working in a liquor store, but she was good about it. And so, after my six weeks as salesclerk, Mother and I had a wonderful trip to Mexico over Thanksgiving. What impressed me the most was how poor the majority of the people were and how richly adorned the Catholic churches were.

Arriving back in Texas I found a telegram from Henry. He had just been discharged from the Army and had returned from Japan on Thanksgiving Eve. I was newly disengaged from Richard, and Henry had dated a fine young woman, sister to his college friend, whom I had encouraged to join the American Red Cross. They knew each other before the war, but this time was under a New Guinea moon. The telegram merely said, "Come to Sheridan, Wyoming on your way home to Ann Arbor."

Well, anyone looking at a U.S. map or the rail route would know that Sheridan is not "on the way." But I put Mother on the train for Michigan, and I headed for Wyoming. Mother said, "Oh, do let me know how things turn out." During a five-hour layover in Kansas City, I had my hair washed and set. I bought a long dress—bright yellow with horizontal stripes of gold thread! I told both the beautician and the sales lady of the coming encounter. I boarded the train once again, overnight to Alliance, Nebraska then to Gillette, Wyoming, and just at dusk on December 8, 1945 we pulled into Sheridan. Unashamedly, I admit there wasn't one passenger who did not know about this remarkable reunion to be.

How would we greet each other? A handshake, perhaps? With the big white dress box in hand I stepped off the train and there he was! We looked into each other's eyes and he blurted out, "What have you got that box in the way for?" Laughingly I flung it aside and we were in each other's arms. As the train pulled away I looked at its windows full of smiling faces, waves and kisses.

We drove down Main Street in Sheridan just as the evening settled in, Christmas lights glittering on new fallen snow. People hurried along the street with packages, cars bustled by. I spied the telegraph office and told Henry I must stop. I sent to Mother: "I'm here and all is well."

We drove to the Burgess home, also on Main Street. Henry's father immediately wanted to clear up a few points. "Are you a Republican or Democrat? You seem to smoke a lot." He was the district judge of three counties and also a rancher. The NX (NX Bar) was the name of the ranch and the brand of its cattle. I received a warm welcome from both of Henry's parents.

We had a thrilling week of rediscovery and romance. Hank was also rediscovering his hometown after five and a half years in the service. He introduced me to the local ice cream parlor, to Hot Tamale Louis's, and to sledding down Linden Hill. We stayed with his family. Henry's father smoked cigars. I was aware of the fact he and Mrs. Burgess disapproved of cigarettes, so every morning Henry and I would saunter downtown and have coffee, and I would have a cigarette or two. I was an avid smoker. After about four days his father took Henry aside and said, "When are you going to ask her to marry you? I'll ask her to marry you if you don't." Henry was tickled.

The next morning Henry announced, "Think I'll take Mary riding at the NX. We'll go to Deer Creek." Sounded good to me, but his parents were aghast, as it was already snowing and temperatures were hovering in the low teens. I was bundled into someone's long underwear and baggy Levi's and away we went. We drove the thirty miles to the Burgess ranch through barren hills blanketed in snow. Mounted on horses, we took off amongst light flurries. By mid-morning the storm was raging. We got off our horses and led them up and down shaggy, snaggy hills and dales. How could Hank see where we were going? At length, maybe a good five or six hours in all, an unpainted small house with a barn loomed ahead. Hank knocked on the door and a startled Ben and Irene Shreve opened to white figures in the blizzard. They ushered us into their kitchen parlor, dining, and warming room. This was Deer Creek. Ben worked that part of the NX.

I was chilled to the bone and asked for hot water.

"With tea?" asked Irene.

"Please."

"With whiskey?" asked Ben.

"Please."

'Twas three hours before I woke up on the sofa where I had sipped that welcomed potion, just as Ben entered the house and plunked down on the counter an uncut hind quarter of a steer. "Well, Irene, what kind of meat do you want to cook?" I could not believe my eyes! We had steak, potatoes, and gravy cooked on her wood stove.

We were given a Coleman lantern to light our way up to the attic where there were a couple of beds with bedrolls laid out. The rest was strictly attic. Though we tip toed across the floor to share a bed we stayed bundled in our underwear. Yes, I guess you'd call it "bundling" and that's all.

Next morning was sunny and quiet with Ben declaring it warm at only eight degrees below zero. It was a while before it was imperative that I brave the cold and bare my bottom in the outhouse. We bade the Shreves a fond farewell and mounted our horses for the trek back to the NX. It was only four hours by sunshine, sparkling snow, and a breathtaking view of the Big Horn Mountains. That night Hank proposed. It dawned upon me slowly that the NX had been a test. Can you beat that? Anyway, I was still of a notion about my second-date remark and accepted with pleasure and anticipation.

I went right home, but it was an arduous trip. Returning to Ann Arbor by train, I had an overnight layover in Lincoln, Nebraska where I had a lovely visit with a professor of violin at the University of Nebraska, whom I had known as one of the members of Glenn Miller's band in London and Paris. Then there was a four hour wait late evening in Chicago. Soldiers filled the trains and I was lucky to get a seat. It is hard to imagine that big gloomy station overflowing with returning soldiers. Talk about being lonely in the midst of a crowd. Mother met me at the beautiful stone depot in Ann Arbor. This was a few days before Christmas and the wedding date was already set: January 19, 1946. A busy, happy time of preparation.

Mother said only, "Oh, this is a dream come true," to which I laughed and replied, "But, Mother, that is *my* line!" Guess I finally knew that this marriage of Mary's to one of whom Daddy had heartily approved long years before was a great relief to Mother. Hank and Daddy had met briefly in Seattle in 1941 and again in Leyte, The Philippines.

Hank had acquired a brand new Ford and called from Coldwater, Michigan just to say he'd be in Ann Arbor shortly. He sounded so abrupt I wondered if he still wanted to marry me. I was to learn that he is always abrupt on the phone.

Henry did indeed want to marry me. He was put in the guest room and I snuck in there the night before we were married, and we carried on a bit. Then he said, "You know, we have to save the real thing until we're married. We've waited all these years; we can wait one more night." We did.

I could not find a wedding dress that I liked so I borrowed Margery's, who is at least two sizes smaller than I am. I don't know how I ever got into it. It was shorter, too, so I wore flat, white satin bedroom slippers. Calla lilies were my choice for my bouquet. Henry's father was his best man.

Our wedding took place on a snowy night at eight thirty. The St. Andrews Boys' Choir preceded us. My attendants were Elizabeth, Margery, and Betty Chapman. My beautiful little flower girl was Ellen Pearson. I did not wear my glasses, so I walked up the aisle on Ralston's arm in a fairylike haze of music, flowers, and candles.

Only much later did Henry tell me his thoughts: the paratroopers signal to jump is a red light. The organist's signal for the wedding march was a red light. Henry noted that red light.

On our wedding day, Mother said to me, "I feel so inadequate about what advice I should be giving but I will try."

"Anything you do, uh, in bed is all right."

"Always be a willing partner. I mean, don't say you have a headache unless you really do."

"Try not to use sex as a weapon."

"It is better to sleep in the same bed, because that makes it easier to patch quarrels."

"If it is possible, it is better for a wife to have a bit of money of her own, so that when she has a real need to buy a pretty hat she won't feel guilty taking it out of the grocery budget."

Betty; Margery; Mary; Elizabeth; and Harriet Pratt, my college roommate

Leaving for our honeymoon

Our honeymoon was at The Farm. Henry had the brand new little Ford, and as we drove to The Farm it made terrible sounds. But if we went fast enough it didn't make any sound at all. Next morning Henry discovered that my brother Ralston had filled the hubcaps with stones. We had a proper welcoming at The Farm: champagne and sandwiches in the icebox, butter on the toilet seat, and bells under the bed.

Because we were the first ever to spend any time in the winter out there, we experienced the one coal-fired floor heater. There was a nice fireplace that we used a great deal, but we stood by the heater warming our front sides, then our back sides. There was a pump for water at the kitchen sink, and we heated water on the stove for our coffee or whatever. We had a beautiful crystal pitcher—a wedding present. The first time we used it I poured boiling water in it and it broke; great tears.

Memorable conversations come to mind.

Henry on our honeymoon and forever after: "I'm still so surprised to find myself alive and well and home and married to you. I want to spend every night possible with you for the rest of our lives."

After our first five days at The Farm we returned to Granny's, prior to our honeymoon trip to the East Coast.

Henry: "Oops, oh, ah. I wasn't sure anyone was in the bathroom, and I'm going to bathe."

Mary: "Neither was I; only accidental that we meet. Thought I'd bathe too. But here we are and how exhilarating to see your whole body!"

Henry smiling: "Turn around again and don't be so self conscious. It was just too cold at The Farm."

Mary: "Could anyone believe all that passion without really seeing each other?"

Henry: "We'll make up for that beginning right now."

Mary: "Such laughter. Such joy. May it always be so."

Henry on our honeymoon: "Gosh, honey, I've lost count but let's do it again."

Linda, Henry's brother's wife, told me during our honeymoon, "If you think marriage is good now, wait ten years—with all that practice, and rough edges smoothed down."

We lived at The Farm the first year Henry was in law school, since every corner of Ann Arbor was filled with students returning from the war. I took a job as a secretary until morning sickness overwhelmed me. As we had only one car, I spent many days alone. I decided I might as well learn how to iron shirts and make bread. I read a lot of books.

Mary: "Isn't it spacious here at The Farm? We don't see other houses and it is such a pretty valley."

Henry, from Wyoming: "It gives me claustrophobia."

Mary: "I cannot can any more tomatoes. It makes morning sickness last all day."

Mary, bursting into the law library in tears: "The doctor says I have RH negative and we will be lucky to have two babies."

Henry: "Let's see. It will take me two and a half years to finish law school. We should be able to get back to Wyoming with two children."

Mary: "Hank, you can't go to your final exam with such fever and chills and weakness from your malaria bout."

Henry: "Yes I can. I won't get well until I do.

Henry: "You are so grouchy. What are you doing all day?"

Mary: "Learning how to iron shirts and make bread, and reading Sinclair Lewis."

Henry: "Ah, he would make anyone grouchy. Perhaps you can find something else to read."

Mary when Henry comes home to The Farm at night from the law library: "I am terrified. The wind makes that branch scratch the roof. The window shudders."

Henry: "What are you reading?"

Mary: "Mysteries."

We had some wonderful parties with other law students recently home from the war and their wives. We served cold cuts or spaghetti and made salads. We were all on an even basis, because we knew all of us received only $90 a month on the GI Bill.

When Henry came back from the library at night and I'd be chattering, he'd say, "Mary, I'm going to have to go back to the library if you don't keep quiet." So I would bury myself once more in a book. But we did spend a lot of time talking about the war, all of his experiences and mine. We got a lot said that was cathartic for both of us.

In the middle of a night, Henry grabbed me and said, “Mary, get in the foxhole. The Japs are coming!” I said, “No, they’re not Japs; they’re Germans!”

After our first year of marriage, we moved to Pittsfield Village, a development of cozy apartments. It was mostly filled with married students. As we visited around Pittsfield, Henry loved to talk about Wyoming. One Sunday noon we had three calls from three wives. Their husbands would not carve the baked chickens. Would Hank please come carve?

We invited a law student and his wife for dinner. We’d brought home antelope from Wyoming and when we sat down to eat, this young man, Peter, asked, “What are we eating? I thought antelope was a bird.” But…Henry had acquired the largest flat-brimmed cowboy hat he could find, which would give the greatest shade. Henry proudly showed Peter his new felt hat, and Peter asked, “What are you doing with a parson’s hat?”

Another time, I was identified in a group of women as the one from Wyoming because I wore trousers!

I felt that Henry and I were lucky in that we came more or less from the same educational and economic background, but we missed the mark on how to celebrate the holidays. Henry’s father never wanted to celebrate Christmas, because his mother had died on Christmas. I always thought Henry would naturally clean the garage because Daddy did, but Henry didn’t because mostly it was my stuff.

But as for values, the Burgess and Hayden families were right in tune, and our parents would have agreed on many issues. Of course Daddy didn’t get to know them, but I’m thankful he knew Henry. One time I kidded Henry soon after we were married and said, “I don’t know about that, I might divorce you.” Henry whipped around and said, “Don’t ever use that word, even in a joking conversation. It is not in our vocabulary or our thoughts.” This doesn’t mean that sometimes Henry and I didn’t have our moments of great anger towards each other. But there is a little anger in every marriage. How can it not be so?

Henry: "Don't be so demonstrative—not even in front of our families. What we are to each other is only for each other."

Mother: "Henry, perhaps you could pick me up when you take Mary to the hospital for this baby."

Henry: "No, Betty, I'd rather it be just Mary and me. I will call you right away.

May 28, 1947, 3:00 p.m. "You have a fine redheaded son."

Mary: "Oh, Henry, since I was thirteen, married or not, boy or girl, I have wanted to name my first born Sheridan, and I cannot help it if you come from a town by that name. Sheridan Samuel Burgess. And we have a Sam on each side of our families. Isn't he beautiful?"

Me to hospital roommate: "Don't these babies look different each time we see them?"

Roommate: "Yes, I think mine has a tinge of red hair."

Nurse, rushing in: "Stop! Stop! I gave you each other's baby. I'm sorry."

Mother: "It is not unnatural to be depressed, Mary. A baby is a great disciplinarian and simply demands routine."

Mary: "You mean we cannot go to the cocktail party because it is time for me to nurse the baby?"

Mother: "Of course you are exhausted if you listen to baby noises all night. And yes you can put him in the other room with the door closed. By the time you hear him cry he will have gotten his proper exercise."

Henry: "I know how tired you are. I'll do the dishes and mop the floor."

Mother: "Once you are sure you have not stuck him with a diaper pin, a baby cries usually because he is too hot or too cold or too wet and messy or is hungry or simply wants to be held."

Henry: "I love to watch you nurse our baby."

Henry in the middle of the night, elbowing me: "Your baby is crying."

Mary: "Oh my, this is the third time I've doused my watch while bathing Sheridan. I'm through wearing it."

Henry: "My dear, you are often not on time with a watch, so it probably won't make any difference."

Henry: "If Sheridan does not like mashed peas do not give them to him. We are not going to quarrel with our children over food."

Mother: "Sometimes they (babies) have to cry themselves to sleep. Give him ten minutes before you pick him up again."

Mary: "Hank, you do not seem to be the same man I married. You are a Father."

Henry: "And you seem to spend all your time with that baby. You have nursed for five months now and cannot seem to get pregnant. You've given him a good beginning; if we are going to have trouble, we'd better start another baby now."

Doctor to me at pre-natal check up: "This test shows you are RH positive. They just had not perfected the test."

Mary: "Now you tell me!"

Henry: "Mary, if I don't make it as a lawyer is it all right with you if we go back to Wyoming and just ranch?"

Mary: "Oh, Hank I'm so proud of you for graduating from the Michigan Law School in this two and a half year stepped-up program. But it seemed like forever. When we get to Wyoming can we have more than one pot and one pan?"

Henry: “Yes, and now let’s buy a truck at the Detroit factory. You can move into 1530 Hill with your mother and Granny while I take all our things to Wyoming, sell the truck and find us a place to live. Then I’ll be back in time for the birth.”

Henry is back and we are waiting for the birth: “Maybe I could learn to play bridge. Granny really likes to win any card game doesn’t she?”

Mary: “So do you.”

Henry: “Well, Betty, here we are off in the night again. I’ll call you right away. If this baby is a girl I want her named Mary Helen.”

Mary to the Registrar at the hospital: “Last year it was $2.50. How come this baby costs $3.95?”

Registrar: “Administration expenses have gone up.”

Henry: “I guess we can afford it. With hospital insurance and these resident doctors, that’s all it costs.”

Mary to the Doctor: “Why, Jim Kreger, you can’t deliver my baby. We used to double date in college.”

Jim: “Hah, I’ll show you. Turn over so we can put the needle in for caudal.”

Mary: “This baby is coming out of my back. That is where the pain is.”

Jim: “July 13, 1948, 6:00 a.m. It is a dark haired girl!”

Mary: “I am not going to be Old Mary or Big Mary the rest of my life. We will have to call her Molly. Sorry to start you with a nickname, but your Daddy is adamant about your name.”

Henry: “Mary, if you don’t stop crying every time I visit the hospital I just won’t come.”

Mary: “I don’t know why I cry when I’m so pleased. Perhaps it is the caudal or all these stitches, and that no one else can visit. Mother is not even allowed.”

Mary: "I feel like you have absorbed my whole self. You dominate my thought processes. In my struggle to adapt, to accommodate, to live in harmony, my being of twenty-five years has been shaken to the roots. It is like hanging on to a roller coaster. Not even my name is left."

Henry: "That's funny. I have thought the same thing has happened to me. And here in Ann Arbor I feel like Mr. Hayden."

A Young Family

Henry was my world, especially in Sheridan, Wyoming. It was *his* birthplace, growing up place, and coming home place from the war and law school. I knew we would spend our lives together here. Henry loved Wyoming, and I was prepared to love it too.

Our way of life was different "out West." His father, James Harry Burgess, had been born in Austin, Nevada, and had come to Big Horn at the age of five by covered wagon. His mother, Helen Helvey, was from Brenham, Texas. The town itself was different, and his lifelong friends were from Sheridan.

Just the vastness of the land—mostly without trees—and the grandeur of the Big Horn Mountains—always in view because we lived on a hill—awed me, a flatlander from the Midwest.

The Big Horn Mountains from The Divide

Henry himself made my life an adventure everyday; he, and our ever-growing family. Henry was always caught up in his chosen profession, the law. "The law is a jealous mistress." Whoever composed this line knew what I soon learned.

At least some of the attitudes and values there were different. Perhaps this was partly due to the NX ranch being twenty-five miles from town, with only a party line phone, no electricity, a coal stove for heat, and an outhouse. Vast hills surrounded the valleys on the NX. It was farm work and riding the herd. Henry's Uncle Charlie, Charlie Helvey, and his family lived there. Aunt Dorothy washed clothes in an outdoor gas-driven machine. She ironed with a sad iron, swept floors (no vacuum), and mopped the linoleum. The windmill was by the front door. I remember huge owls, almost six feet wing tip to wing tip, and still the vastness of the land, and a long way from a neighbor. None of this was uncommon on the surrounding ranch lands.

Burgess family portrait with two-year-old Henry and ten-year-old Harry, 1920

Henry in front of the barn at the NX, already a good hand

Dad and Helen Burgess, at the Sheridan train depot, September 1949: "Welcome to Sheridan! We don't know how you made that long ride with fourteen-month-old Sheridan and six-week-old Molly in her wicker clothesbasket. She looks so darling in all that pink, but does she scream all of the time?"

Henry: "No. A freight train went by just as they got off the train and I think a cinder is in her eye."

Henry later that day: "Well, here is our little log house I rented for $50 a month. It has a huge heat-o-lator river rock fireplace. The children can be in the bedroom. All hardwood floors, even in the bathroom. Fortunately, the garage is attached to the kitchen, as it will be a nice bedroom for us. The laundry can be in the basement with the coal furnace. That funny thing, as you call it, is a sump pump. Even though we live on this high hill by the fairgrounds there is underground water. It works automatically."

Mary: "How do you expect me to be able to wash dishes when I can lift my eyes to those glorious mountains?"

Henry: "No, you can't have an outdoor thermometer. One look and you'd freeze standing by the fireplace."

Mary: "I miss trees."

Henry: "There are plenty on Loucks Street and in the park."

Henry: "Happy day! I passed the Bar Exam. Now I'll campaign for the State House of Representatives. And I have two rooms for an office, one for me and one for a secretary."

Mary: "Dear Mother, I just put up diapers for two on the line, but it started to rain so they are draped all over the house."

Henry: "Hoot and I just bought a black Labrador puppy for $40. She can live with us and her name is Lucky."

Mary: "Dear Mother, I went out to get the diapers only to discover Lucky has torn them to shreds!"

Henry: "I have gone campaigning door to door in town, at the mines, and in surrounding towns. Now for formal visits to Arvada, Clearmont, and Big Horn, and for other rallies with Mervin and Barbara Champion."

Mary: "What a wonderful way for me to learn about my new home. Love the square dancing."

Henry: "How exciting to have won! We will be in Cheyenne for six weeks, beginning the first week in January."

Mary to a neighbor: "Hank is doing so well in the law practice. The first month he made $13. The second, $42. This third month is $93. That is three dollars more than we got under the GI Bill when in law school. What? Why, how kind of you to share your garden vegetables!"

Mary: "Guess what happened, Henry. I was hanging out the diapers and Sheridan locked me out of the house. He is standing on Molly in the playpen. Can you please come home?"

Russell York, the welder: "Mary, this is the third time you have brought me this old iron crib to mend. May I ask what kind of a child you have?"

Mary: "No, the day didn't go too well. While I was nursing Molly, Sheridan sat on the kitchen table and ate a whole pound of butter.

Mary: It was such a gorgeous sunny day that I took Sheridan for a ride on his sled. I noticed his face was red and I couldn't feel my legs. How was I to know it is sixteen degrees below zero?"

Sheridan and Molly, at 912 Victoria

Mary: "Lucky has chewed up the satin comforter Granny gave us. I'm about to turn her out and she can have any dog's puppies."

Hoot at the house 10 minutes later: "I'll take Lucky. Gotta tear back to work."

Mary: "What a long, cold four days it was while you were elk hunting in the mountains. But I can see that a twelve point elk is something. But he must be the oldest and toughest meat in the world."

Mary: "Dear Mother, I can't believe how diapers freeze on the line even in the sun."

Mother, chuckling: "I can hardly believe this. My train from Ann Arbor being delayed by the blizzard five days in Nebraska. Now sitting on the floor of my daughter's little log nest in the West making a quilt with you. What fun, and Henry at the Plains Hotel in Cheyenne."

Mother, as we mount the steps of the Wyoming State Capitol: “It takes my breath a little as I remember when Daddy and I took you children up these very steps just to show you a state capitol in 1929. And now Henry and you are a part of it.”

Henry: “What an exhilarating experience it has been to be in the legislature. Now I’ll open the door to my law office again and hope somebody brings me some work to do. Meantime, I’m reading all the statutes.”

Judge Burgess: “You know, son, you cannot practice in front of me, but if something comes up I’ll get another judge.”

Henry: “Dad, I filled out this form exactly the way Bill Redle did. You signed his and have made me redo mine.”

Judge Burgess: “Bill’s work will pass but yours is going to be perfect.”

In the fall Henry would go pheasant hunting, bring his quota home, and expect me to pull the feathers out. I did, for a couple of years, hating every minute of this so-called skill. One night I came home from bridge club, quite furious. “What have I done?” asked my guy. The girls had roared with laughter when I asked them how they plucked their pheasants. It seems they only consented to cook the fowl after the same had been properly cleaned, plucked, and dressed by their husbands. Hank was tickled by my earnest effort to please and to be a local wife. But he never pulled that trick again.

Parties. What a partying town. That first spring we attended a cocktail party. I knew only a couple of people, and I found myself talking to a man I did not know. The easiest conversation was to talk about the weather, so I said, “Isn’t this snow in April great?” Henry stood nearby and said to me, “Mary, he doesn’t want this snow because he is lambing.” Oh.

The next man I spoke to—oh, there were a lot of people, bewildering—I said, “Isn’t this storm terrible?” Henry said, “But Mary, he wants the moisture, he grows wheat.” Oh.

It took years to know which people did what and to know, once and for all, that no matter what event was scheduled—a rodeo, 4H, athletic contests, or even haying—rain was always welcome.

When we went to visit the NX, as we passed by another ranch on the way, Henry's father would say, "There is a fine ranch." And I would look down the lane a mile and say, "No matter what the building looks like, at least it has trees," never dreaming that eight years later this would become our Pony Track Ranch. When Dad knew that he was dying of cancer, he insisted that the NX be sold. Henry and his brother Ber, who did not live anywhere nearby, and their Uncle Charlie, who lived on the ranch, were devastated because they all loved it.

Judge Burgess: "As district judge for thirty-three years I have witnessed many bitter feuds among ranch children after the parent or parents die. Henry, you and your brother and Uncle Charlie and your mother all have equity in the NX Ranch. I am going to sell the ranch. You are all friends now, but would not remain such trying to run the NX together after I am gone; nor can any of you afford to buy the other out. If you still want to ranch, go buy your own."

Henry: "Allen Fordyce has purchased the NX. Mary, we have always made decisions together and I apologize for making one without you, but the eight hundred acres east of the NX were up for lease and I couldn't bear to be without land, so I have leased the Weigand Place for one dollar per acre per year. Hoot West and I will raise wheat on it."

I complained of his being away at the Weigand Place, to which Henry replied, "But we are planting, then the wheat grows by itself. A few days to harvest and sell and we'll have a nest egg." I was ensconced with children. At least he was not leaving me to play golf. One day he came home with a beautiful red Buick station wagon and exclaimed, "This is wheat money."

Mary, Sheridan, Henry, and Molly

Henry: "Mary, you are pregnant."

Mary: "Oh, no. What makes you think so?"

Henry: "Last night you were absolutely obsessed with getting potato chips. Besides, your breasts have changed."

Henry: "Betty, it is so nice of you to come to Sheridan again and sleep on our sofa. I'll call as soon as this baby arrives. Come on, Mary."

Mary: "No, wait until I shave my legs."

Mary, in the delivery room: "Do you mean, Dr. Booth, that my feet are not going to reach for the ceiling?"

Louis Booth: "Heavens no. You plant them right here on the table where you can get leverage and help me. Now give me a push as if you might be moving a piano."

Mary: "No caudal?"

Louis: "You can have a whiff of ether if it gets too tough. Push again, I see red hair."

Louis: "July 18, 1950. You have a fine red-headed girl."

Mary, wheeling out of the delivery room: "Oh, Henry, what a welcome sight you are. Your smile is so tender, and this baby is so adorable."

Nurse, on the fourth day: "Now really, Mrs. Burgess, we have to have a name to register.

Mary: "We've been through both families and the name book and we never agree. Okay, Henry. How about Tyler Elizabeth?

Henry: "That's a good one."

Mary: "Quick, nurse, write it down before he changes his mind."

Mary: "We can keep her in the wicker clothesbasket on the table and put her on the floor when we eat."

Henry, days later at home as we gaze at our lovely daughter with her soft red hair and delicate coloring: "How did you get the name Tyler?"

Me, rather proudly: "Well, it is from your side. Your father always admired his stepfather, Jake Taylor. But that sounded so masculine I derived Tyler out of Taylor."

Henry: "Oh, honey, that is all right, but his name was Wagner."

Mary, taking Tyler to Louis for her checkup and shot, dragging Sheridan and Molly: "I did not know one could have a baby and be cheerful too."

It was always a relief to have that first cigarette after my babies were born and find out it tasted good again. Tyler loved to nurse, but whenever I started to rock the old chair, she was quick to complain. Perhaps she got enough rocking before she was born when I would gather up Sheridan and Molly to rock before naps and at bedtime and sometimes in between, when I was too tired to chase them.

Sheridan, Tyler, and Mary

Henry: "Please don't call me on the phone and start by saying: Guess what's happened! My heart always jumps into my throat."

Mary: "Hank, I am merely calling you to say that while Tyler was nursing, Sheridan wandered all over the house with the syrup tin upside down and leaking. While I was cleaning that up Molly dumped all the oranges around the house. While I was picking them up Sheridan found the newly delivered milk bottles and crashed them, glass and all, on our cement-floored garage bedroom. We are all going down to Mops' to survive the rest of the day.

Mary: "Henry, I am merely calling to say Sheridan disappeared for two hours. Somebody found him wandering toward the country club. Don't know how they knew he was ours."

Mary: "Henry, I am merely calling…oh, you actually have a client in the office? Never mind."

Mary: "Sheridan, why are you crying?"

Sheridan: "Because the radio keeps saying, 'This is Sheridan, Wyoming' and my name is Sheridan Burgess."

Mary: "Yes, Mother, I am indeed going to give Sheridan a knife for his third birthday. I don't want to start him on the road to crime or guilty conscience just because he is always stealing the paring knife."

Mother: "Well, if you insist, then I will give him Band-Aids."

Mary: "Hank, I thank you so much for always coming home on time. This day has been so awful you will just have to take over. I'm going to the movies."

Mary: "I'm so happy to have been asked to join this bridge club. We are eleven, so we can always invite an extra. There are six of us pregnant. Who will have a house big enough to hold us?"

Mary: "Oh, how my back hurts; must be from carrying all these babies inside and out. Guess I'll go to your mother's osteopath after all."

Henry: "The 11th Airborne commander, General Swing, and Doug Quandt are coming for pheasant hunting. Let's have a dinner party."

Mary: "Uh, for sixteen in this little house? Okay, somehow I'll get the children to bed early."

Guest: "Sorry, Mary, I spilled my drink in the middle of your bed."

Mops: "I'll help you re-cut these antelope steaks. I think that's gristle, or hide?"

Another Guest: "I was leaning against the refrigerator and something slid down behind."

Mary: "My cherry pies."

Mary: "Oh, General Swing, we have loved having you in our home. I'll find Henry."

Henry in the bathroom: "Sheridan and Molly were both so messy I thought I should give them baths."

Mother: "I'm tired of hearing about diapers on the line. Merry Christmas and Happy Birthday. Here is a dryer."

Mary: "Thank goodness for Kendrick Park. Shade and swings for Molly and Sheridan while I nurse Tyler. It's one hundred and three degrees."

Henry: "Let's build a house big enough for as many children as we want."

Mary: "Hank, I'm going to wheel Tyler in the buggy and see how our new house is coming. Only eight blocks to our 912 Victoria Street."

Carpenter: "Mrs. Burgess, I'm afraid Sheridan and Molly have eaten all our lunches."

Henry: "Wouldn't you know we are moving on the day of what turns out to be our biggest blizzard, March 17, 1951. We won't forget!"

Neighbor: "I'm calling to tell you Tyler is sitting knee deep in mud."

Mary: "Smile, Tyler, I'm taking your picture. Have a good time."

Another neighbor: "I'm calling to say your children are naked in the backyard."

Mary: "Oh, good. It is hot, isn't it?"

Another neighbor: "Someone broke our basement window."

Henry: "We will pay."

Molly and Tyler

Henry, at a party: "Let's go home."

Mary: "I'm not ready to leave the party. Do let's stay."

Henry: "I get so angry when you won't leave. I'm tired and I have to work tomorrow."

Mary: "Goodnight, friends, Henry is waiting in the car."

Mary: "How embarrassing. He really went off and left me."

Henry: "Got half way home, but then knew that I had to get you sooner or later. I tremble I am so mad."

Mary: "Good morning, dear hostess. We had a lovely time last night. When Hank says let's go, I run."

Mary, years later: "Are you ready to go home?"

Henry: "Let's stay awhile longer."

Mary: "When did we cross paths?"

Henry: "I can hardly wait to get into bed with you."

Mary: "Merry Christmas. A Ping-Pong table. Wonderful for winter with the children. I grew playing it on boats and in France."

Mary: "Ping-Pong again, Hank? It's ten p.m. and I'm exhausted.

Henry, eventually: "Well, I finally beat you."

Mary: "Gee, we haven't played Ping-Pong in an age. Why, Henry Burgess, do you mean to say all I had to do was let you win?"

Mary: "Sheridan! Molly! Get off of the roof this minute!"

Molly: "I'm scared. I can't get down."

Mary: "I'll climb out the window and get you."

Mary to neighbor: "Can you hear me? Please help. I'm frozen with fright. Can't get my feet out of the gutter. No, don't call the fire department."

Molly, who had gotten down on her own: "Mommy, what are you doing up there? I can see your panties! I can see your panties!"

Henry: "Laying a few bricks in the driveway each evening, sprinkling water on the sand and cement mixture. I'll eventually get it done."

Mary: "If we ever find a ranch and move I won't find it hard to leave this house but will miss the trees and bushes and garden we've worked so hard to establish."

Mother: "It doesn't matter how large your basement playroom is, because children will not be happy unless they are under your feet."

Mary: "Mother, why don't you visit longer? You have come so far."

Mother: "Because this is as long as I can keep my mouth shut."

Mary on Sunday morning, May 1951, screaming: "There is terrible pain somewhere in my belly!"

Henry: "Thanks, Louis, for coming right over. Mary just hasn't gotten around to telling you she is pregnant."

Louis, looking out our bedroom window: "Mary, do you realize that you literally threw me out of the room when I tried to examine you?"

Mary: "Did I? Don't remember a thing."

Louis: "Perhaps it is a tubular pregnancy. Now don't get upset. You won't have this baby, but can have others. Whatever it is, I must operate this morning."

Henry: "Betty, would you mind unpacking your bags?"

Mary, waking up from anesthesia: "Oh, Henry, how wonderful to see your face. Why are you smiling?"

Henry: "You still have our baby. You had three ovarian cysts and one had burst which caused your pain. Louis cut the cysts out. You are intact."

Mary: "Louis, now that I'm huge, look at my stitches down my belly. They are two and a half inches wide."

Louis: "Well, nobody's going to see them except Henry and me. We don't care."

Mary: "Louis, is it still all right for us to make love? Even at eight months along?"

Louis: "Certainly, as long as you can manage. You can't hurt the baby."

Mary: "I'm not going to the hospital until I see the osteopath first. My aching back!"

Dr. Grange, the osteopath: "Just tell me when the contractions come and I'll work in between. I don't mind getting up at night."

Mary: "Henry, I guess this is one trip I cannot change my mind about, can I?"

Louis, early morn, December 21, 1951: "You have a fine dark-haired daughter."

Mary, wheeling out of the delivery room: "Oh, Henry, so very good to see you right here. I know, she looks like a Helvey. I cannot keep on having babies just to get one to look like me."

Mary to herself: "Heather Hayden Burgess. So beautiful. How can I keep on loving each one more and more? I guess I'll really have to succumb to motherhood. Thank you, Hank, for letting me come home to open stockings on Christmas Day. But I'm so glad to sink back into bed at the hospital. Molly, dear, I'm glad you are glad to have me home again, but stop biting my legs. Ah, the quiet of night nursing. A drink, some cigarettes, a good book, and Heather, all snuggled in the old rocking chair. But in the daytime, fending off three others who want to sit on my lap, too. Have to push them away with feet as well as hands."

Mary: "Hank, wake up, what is all the banging?"

Henry: "A fire in the basement! I closed the door again. I'll phone the fire department and get the two children upstairs. You get the others downstairs!"

Mary to herself: No time to argue with Henry, but we have three children upstairs. I'll follow him. Oh, he is right. There are only two upstairs; I'll go back down."

Henry: "I don't think the operator got my full message. We'll call when I get Sheridan and Molly across the street. Take Tyler and Heather next door."

Mary to herself: A baby under each arm. Hmmm, six diapers will do and shoes for Tyler. Here I am standing beneath our neighbor's window where we had supper tonight. I cannot think of her name, so how can I call to her? Hope the snow stops coming down. Boy, the fire engine is quick. Oh yes: Tad! "Tad, please let us in."

Henry: "The insurance people are coming this morning. I have to go to the office."

Mary: I must keep things normal for the children. I'll make cherry pies, then I'll nurse Heather in the rocking chair in the living room. "Oh, yes, you people just go down to the basement."

Insurance Man: "Mary, you should not be in the living room as the floor might fall in. Lots of debris under the fireplace where there was no asbestos covering."

Kay Neard, telephone operator: "No, Henry, I didn't get your name or address, but I recognized your voice."

Mary: "Hank, the only thing that is missing is our whole drawer of silver."

Henry: "Gosh, isn't that disappointing to think someone took advantage."

Mary, several days later: "Guess what? The silver drawer is in the garden. I don't think anything is missing."

Henry: "Oh? Oh. Uh, I seem to recall now taking it out myself."

Molly: "I love holding Heather. This is my baby."
Mary: "Why do you say it like that?"
Molly: "Because she has dark hair just like mine."

Visitor: "What pretty red hair your children have."
Mary whispering: "Okay, now tell Molly what pretty eyes she has or something."
Visitor: "Molly, your eyes are a beautiful blue."
Mary: "Hank, I think I've found out why Molly is always so embarrassing when we have company. She was an angel today."

Mary: "We are off to a party so—Goodnight, Sheridan and Molly and Tyler and Heather. Now go back into the kitchen to finish supper—we've kissed all around."
Henry: "What are you doing out on the front steps in your slip?"
Mary: "Don't worry, I'm putting my gray velvet on immediately. I just couldn't let all those sticky little hands get on my dress."

Mary: "It seems you are always at the Weigand Place every weekend and I'm left at home with the children."
Henry: "But we are working the ground and planting winter wheat. It would be nice if you brought a lunch out."
Mary: "Well, here we are with a picnic. Good thing I brought the playpen. The cattle surely like to stand under the only big shade tree on these eight hundred acres, out of the hot, hot sun."
Henry: "I love seeing my family out here. Sheridan, don't wander too far—don't know where the rattlers are."
Mary, on another trip to the Weigand Place with all the children: "How far is it as the crow flies?"
Sheridan (five years old): "How does a crow fly?"
Mary: "Well, uh, it is the shortest distance between two points."
Sheridan in disgust: "Oh no, Mother, a crow flies with wings."

Mary, to Mary: I am nothing but a brood mare. This is my home. It must be my castle, also. My center. So I should find things to do right here that will content me. There must be something more than herding small children and all that goes with it. I cannot keep on hiding by joining organizations and going to ladies luncheons and singing in the choir just so I can sit down for one whole hour and not hear a scream or a cry or a squabble or change yet another diaper. See my garden? See the clothes I've made? See the furniture I've refinished? Oh, my back aches so much.

Henry: "Well, dear, we certainly know the whole countryside with all these drives we take to lull a baby to sleep, to let us sit awhile and give the children a change of view."

Mailman at door: "Mary, how can you let those children run around without any clothes on when it is twenty below?"

Mary: "If they want to pretend they are jumping into a pool on a hot day by jumping off the sofa, that's fine with me. What else?"

Mary to neighbor: "Thanks for having me over for a cup of coffee and a cigarette. I can watch our house in case it starts burning or a child leaves. I'm sure the children often quarrel just to see whose side I'll take. They won't be fighting when I return."

Mary: "Henry, why do you have to go to the office every night?"

Henry: "How do you think we are going to pay for the children's education?"

Mary: "Oh, yes, of course. Sheridan *will* be in kindergarten soon."

Henry; "What are all those books you are reading by Dr. Gesell?"

Mary: "I've got to find out why Molly is suddenly so impossible."

Henry: "Sheridan now has a teacher and kindergarten class. That is what Molly is missing and needs. Isn't there a dancing school that will take four-year-olds?"

Molly: "Is it Tuesday again and I get to go to my dancing class? Goody."

Mary: "Hank, here I've been studying these child behavior books for weeks and yet you come up with the right answer, just like that. How exasperating, but what a relief to know that you know, wise man."

Mary: The neatest aspect of kindergarten is for Sheridan to finally realize that it isn't just his mother who tries to make him behave. The teacher seems to have the same idea, and all his little friends have to behave also. Thanks be.

Henry: "Here is a beautiful Sunday, all the children are well and we are having a happy lunch in the backyard. Why are you so grumpy, Mary?"

Mary: "It is Mother's Day and you have not even said a word about it."

Henry, with a glint in his eye: "Honey, you are not my mother."

Henry: "It says right here in the statute that it is against the law to gamble or to engage in prostitution. Now that I've been elected county attorney, I have told the sheriff his first job is to close it all up. He is not a bit happy. It is my job to conform to the law, to make it work. I am not a reformer. If the law is changed then that is fine with me."

Clara: "Henry, I am a waitress at the Fern Cafe and I want to warn you to keep Mary and the children safe. So many gamblers and dealers come in for coffee and I hear of the dire things they want to do to you."

Henry: "I've just been offered two thousand dollars a month to leave the gambling alone.

Mary: "While you were at the office tonight I turned off our lights and opened the window before getting into bed. The evening was soft and the streets so quiet. Then a car slowed by our house and the air was splintered with the crash of something thrown on our sidewalk, then the car sped away. It was a whole case of shattered beer bottles. Can't let the children out barefooted any more."

Henry: "Retaliation for shutting down the gambling, I think."

Henry: "The true wealth of the West lies in the land."

Henry: "In my job as county attorney I see a parade of people on the down side of life. How joyous was my week's job at Boy's State! All the wonderful talented youngsters there are. I had almost forgotten because the only boys I see as county attorney are in trouble or are troublesome."

Mother and Henry in later years, the week of Molly's wedding

Leaving Town Life Behind

We had built our house for many children in town. We were putting up wallpaper. Henry wanted to look at a ranch. For seven years we had been looking for the right ranch. He had stated, "We need a ranch that's big enough to support a hired man year around, close enough to town so I can practice law, and something we can eventually pay for." Even so, I didn't know what "right" meant to Henry. I'd see a nice house with a few acres and he'd say, "No, no. That's not what I mean."

One day Henry called me up from the office and said there was a ranch up for sale and we should go look at it right away, but "first I want to go to the courthouse and find out what the water rights are."

The records showed that the first water rights were issued in 1884. Sunday morning we took the older children to Sunday school and three-year-old Sarah went with us to visit that ranch on Lower Prairie Dog Creek, the one his father had admired.

They didn't have a telephone, so we drove out and Henry went to the door and knocked. A man with a belligerent look on his face opened the door. This was during the hunting season and Adam

Goodman did not want to have more hunters. But when Henry told him why he was there, he was wreathed in smiles and Henry waved for me to come in. Anna Goodman took me through the house and Adam took Henry to see a few pastures. When we were going back to the car, I looked up to make sure those mountains were still in sight. They were, right from the house. Without going back for a second look, by Thursday we signed the papers.

I said, "You know Henry, I think we should do something about the bathroom in the house." He said, "Bathroom? Where is the bathroom? The first thing I want to do is take out one of the fences in the back." It was a while before I learned that ranch couples were ever balancing what *she* wanted to do to the house and what *he* wanted to do to the land.

We moved to the ranch on December 20 and the next day we had a birthday party for Heather. Everyone was thrilled, particularly Sheridan. Henry's Dad would have approved. Christmas Day we had a family of three come out for dinner. Henry disappeared for a while, and when he came back he brought onto the porch a Welsh pony-horse crossbreed. I have a wonderful picture of all five of the children sitting on "Thunder." Wish I could find it.

Our hired man turned out to be Adam Goodman's nephew, Walter Goodman. While Walter and Henry were interviewing each other, Henry said, "Well, you've been on very strict hours working on an oil rig. There are no set hours on the ranch. You might have to be up early and stay up late." Walter said he understood that and added, "By the way, the woman doesn't want to have any part of doing anything on the ranch." He was hired.

There was a little house on the ranch, about two miles away, where Walter's family lived. His children and our children went to the one room country school, which was a couple of miles down the road. There were four of ours, two of his, and four or six others—maybe fifteen with one teacher.

Mrs. Goodman left the ranch house itself scrupulously clean, but out the back door and towards the creek the garbage had been dumped for fifteen years. She was always dismayed at where they had dumped the garbage. It took Henry a while to get up his nerve to tell Walter that his first job would be cleaning up the garbage. All through the years we would find things that had been dumped there. We started a dump in a draw where Henry didn't want any more erosion, at least a mile and a half from the house.

The first few years we could make the ranch payments with the sale of our wheat crop. Then the price dropped so low that it wasn't worth putting it up.

With the house every day was pretty much a surprise. The living room was wallpapered in brown—brown flowers and brown feathers—with a maroon carpet. All the other rooms had linoleum floors, even the dining room. Half of the kitchen linoleum was something to stumble over and we kept tacking it down. Later, when we had the floors refinished, in every room there was a large brown spot that would not budge. A previous family had left with big candles burning, fumigating for some contagious disease. Diphtheria, I believe.

Henry and I slept in the bedroom right off of the kitchen, and there was a tiny, high window. Our bed was right under the tiny window. One night I had a tingling feeling, and again the next night. It was snowing. The flakes came through the window and fell on my face.

There was a trap door in front of the toilet. It was stuffed with straw to keep the pipes from freezing. Well, they froze anyway. Henry went to town and got a burner and brought it out and set it down in there. Until the pipes defrosted, I sat and watched that the straw didn't catch fire.

Part of an 1884 homestead, the house sat on a bank overlooking Lower Prairie Dog Creek. Much of the soil protecting the house had eroded away. We were forever propping and patching, and also adding to the house. Later we leased and then bought a ranch about seven miles down the road, the WS Ranch. That's where Sheridan still lives.

Jamie came home from college and lived with us for ten years. He lived in a little cottage next to the house, so he had a bit of independence, but he came in for meals and visits. We always said that if he married, we'd move off the ranch.

* * *

We were excited about our first calf crop. We were just becoming acquainted with our all-around man, Walter Goodman. The three of us were in the corral contemplating a newborn that could not get off his knees. I said, "The trouble with this calf is his tendons are too short." Henry said, "Hush, Mary, you don't know anything about cattle." The next day we had the vet out for another problem. I asked him, "By the way, what do you think is wrong with this little fellow?" He said, "The trouble with this calf is that his tendons are to short."

* * *

One day in January, in seven degrees below zero, Henry and I headed for the hills on horseback. The snow was soft and new and I felt our horses walking tip-toe as the snow packed their frogs. Our job was to gather the last of the heifers to come down for winter feeding. Walter would join us later with the pickup and sandwiches I'd made before the children left for their one room school. It was seven or eight miles just to reach The Divide. Henry directed me to a point out yonder and told me to look down both sides of the canyon for wandering heifers. I really didn't want to look for fear I'd find some. Well, I did. Four of them. So down my gelding, Birney, and I went, into the steep draw.

I learned that young cattle don't herd well. Birney got so exasperated he would nip their rumps. We were on a steep slope and I decided to take this opportunity to "go." I was wearing long johns, jeans, and the stiff new chaps Henry had had made to measure for my Christmas present. Plus the heavy leather jacket, also a Christmas gift. I knew I would need a high place or a rock to saddle up again, once I'd gotten all those clothes down then back up again. Birney was patient but my first try to remount was not a success. So I just sat down in a snow bank and contemplated the vast expanse of land. I had been alone for three hours. Actually I was contemplating thus: Other wives work in their husband's store, or are their secretaries, or maybe cook in the family restaurant; lots of ways to be a helpmate. How many are sitting in a snowbank thinking about young cows being the enemy? At least it had warmed to twenty degrees.

I finally lowered the stirrup and hoisted myself up. I was riding the flat saddle I'd grown up riding—English saddle, if you like. I found I could cowgirl that way as well as I could on a western saddle. Midafternoon Birney and I actually made it up the canyon to the pickup with all four girls. Sandwiches! I clambered into the vehicle and was about to take a bite when galloping over, Henry called, "Your heifers are getting away!" "Oh?" say I. Henry smiled and said he'd take care of them.

* * *

One day I marveled, "How could Henry let me drive a tractor straight at him to get as close to the creek as possible to dump some riprap?" Henry had commandeered the old Coffeen Street bridge and had had it dumped at the ranch. I didn't know how to drive a tractor. I might have run over him or simply shoved him into the creek. "Faith in a wife."

* * *

There was a knock on the door and I found Bob, our veterinarian, standing in the doorway. He said, "Is Walter here? Is anyone here but you?" I said, "No, I'm the only one." He looked at me critically and said, "Well, I guess you'll do. Come down to the corral with me…I want you to hold this nose twitch, a loop of hemp that is tied to make a handle with the loop. I'm going to put this over the horse's nose and you hold it and when I tell you to twist, you twist as hard as you can and stay clear of the horse's hooves. The idea is that when he is worried about his nose, I will give him a shot in the rump." I performed my duty well. Bob said thank you and drove away. I went back to the kitchen to continue stirring a pot on the stove.

* * *

Riding in the pastures and hills I found clean, sun-baked animal bones. I began to collect: the skull of a horse electrocuted by lightning—beautiful; then cattle skulls, spines, pelvises, and leg bones; skulls of coyotes and beavers.

Moving cattle with Henry, I got off my horse four times to retrieve four tiny prairie dog skulls, the only time in thirty-five years that I found them.

* * *

Henry and I were riding the Coutant Creek pasture, gathering the last of the bulls. Henry had gone ahead with a number of bulls and I was rounding up the last one. I turned around to make sure there were no more. There weren't, but when I went back to the one I had, he had completely disappeared. Too far to yell for Henry. I looked around the creek and back into the hills where we had been; he simply wasn't to be found. Nearby, there was a completely disintegrated homestead, with a hole where the cistern had been. I looked down the hole and there was the bull looking up at me. He had simply dropped through. I galloped ahead and flagged Henry down who came back and looked and laughed, saying, "Well, we're just going to have to get him out somehow." Henry rode back to the ranch to get the tractor with the shovel on the front. He returned to scoop out the side of the hole, whereupon the bull walked grandly up to the ground level and joined the others.

* * *

We call one whole area of the ranch "The Divide," an extensive area of high hills edging the back of the ranch. Henry wanted to check out a spring on The Divide, so we drove over the top and started down toward the spring. It was very muddy and steep and the light pickup we were in tilted over onto its side. Again, Henry had to go back to the ranch to get another vehicle to pull the pickup upright. When Henry came back, I stayed in with the motor running, so I could back it out once he pulled it out. This was in the days before seatbelts and Henry said, "Now, if this starts to turn over with you, be on the side that is tipping on you." To my great relief it came back upright and I gave her the gun backwards until we were safely up on top once more.

Whatever I was asked to do, it was new to me. Henry wanted to move some cows with their calves from one pasture to another. And I was to be the holding pen, not letting anything through the gate unless Henry had ascertained it was a pair. While he was gathering some cattle, I pointed out to Henry a pair I'd been watching. He said, "No." I said, "How can you tell, I've been studying them." "Well," he said, "You're looking at the wrong end. That's a steer."

Sometimes I was not as fast as I should have been because I was concerned about keeping my horse out of prairie dog holes. I should have had more faith in my horse. He didn't want to go into a prairie dog hole, either. Occasionally we lost a very young horse to having a foot caught in one of these and breaking its leg. Of course, it had to be shot.

Ranch chores with Walter. At least I was a good truck driver from Red Cross days.

One time when I was acting as a holding pen, the cows were fussing around making sure their calves were with them. As I studied them, they began to look like they were at a ladies' meeting. I could visualize a flowered hat on one lady who was in charge, and then of course there was always one who was meek and mild in the background. They all took on their own personalities.

Henry taught me how to yell at the cattle, urging them up the hillside or wherever they are supposed to go. There is a certain way to save your vocal chords. "Ha! Hop! Ho!" Sometimes when we were trailing and I didn't really want to yell I would say, "Poop poo pa dupe!" or "Betty Boop!" or some other nonsense phrase. It was a long time before I realized that one didn't really have to yell at the cows at all. You might say, "Shhtt! Shhtt!" to keep them going, or simply be behind them. They don't really like going straight up a hill. They would rather meander up it or waft back and forth. The ideal way to trail cattle is to let them go one behind another and take their own pace.

Branding the calves always took several people and much effort. First, a rider would rope the calf by the hind hooves and drag it to a pair of wrestlers, who would up-end it and hold it down. Someone castrated, someone branded, someone vaccinated, and someone pasted the horns, which hurts the calves—that was the hardest part, but better than dehorning them later. Then we would have to keep the calves away from their mothers so the pasting would take effect. One year I did the branding. I wasn't asked to do it again, because I didn't leave the iron on long enough, and for half of them the brand didn't take.

Henry dragging a calf out of the pen to the wrestlers at a branding. George Pearson, leaning against the gate, tallying heifers and steers.

Smoke rises as the brand is applied

Henry found some money in fifteen-year-old Sheridan's room and wondered where it came from. Sheridan proudly said he earned it up in Otter Creek, Montana, bull riding.

Henry suggested polo. "That's a sissy's game," said Sheridan. "Try it, " Henry insisted. Sheridan found out it isn't for sissies.

The Moncrieffe Polo Field in Big Horn was the second oldest in the country. The players were looking for young recruits. We bought Sheridan polo mallets, a used flat saddle, and the best polo helmet.

Thus began thirty years of centering our Sundays and practice days on polo. Sheridan used our Thoroughbred ranch horses. When Jamie was twelve, he joined his brother on the polo field.

It's Always Something

Sarah

On a cold, clear evening in April, 1960, all eight of us had attended a party at the Wyarno Community Hall and were driving home. The moon was full and the hills glowed with its reflection. Sarah stared at the moon and asked, "What is it like to die?" I suppose I answered, as anyone might to one who has barely turned four, that it is like going to sleep and never waking up again.

But that did not happen to her until the afternoon of June 7 in the same year. In the meantime she glowed enchantingly at Easter in a new lavender dress. Her tonsils and adenoids came out and she started eating all sorts of foods she'd always refused—roughage, mostly, which must have hurt her touchy throat. She had rickets. When I stopped nursing at five months we discovered she could not tolerate any sort of milk. Louis Booth said to put 7-UP, well shaken, in her bottle. "Fortunately people survive without milk," he said. She was three before we could wean her from 7-UP, and milk was okay by then.

So at last she was on a proper diet, growing well, happily basking in the love of her older brother and three sisters and lovingly bossing her younger brother. From the time he was born she was careful that I did not give him any unnecessary love or attention, and I was careful to give him none in her presence.

She and I played the new Mitch Miller records together. Riding in the car or going to bed, she always demanded that I sing "My Bonnie Lies Over the Ocean," "Polly Wolly Doodle," "Old Kentucky Home," or "Goodnight Ladies"—songs my father had sung to me in his rich tenor when I was her age.

Sarah Louise Burgess

Heather and Sarah

Early June was very hot that year. The children often played in the creek, shallow and silty by the bridge. They cooled off, hunted for tiny seashells, and came up to the house for baths to wash off the mud. Sarah never went further than putting one foot gingerly in the water. None of Lower Prairie Dog Creek was over a foot and a half deep where they played, and I knew this was where Sarah, Heather, and Tyler were going to be that early afternoon. I put Jamie into his crib for a nap and stretched out gratefully on the sofa and fell into a deep sleep. I was wearing pink shorts and a hand-me-down man's pink shirt, and was barefoot.

Coming out of my heavy sleep I could hear Heather: "Mother, Mother, wake up. Sarah is dead."

Me, coming out of oblivion: "Oh, no, she must be only sleeping."

Heather: "I know when things are dead and she is. Down by the flume."

"The flume! Why that is a half mile away."

We dashed to the station wagon and I called to Sheridan and Walter who were working in the old shop. We drove up a hill and down to the left—perhaps a half or three quarters of mile from the house. By that time our irrigator, Henry Lackman, had put Sarah on top of the muddy tarps in the back of his pickup. Tyler was nowhere to be found. I was startled to discover another young boy and girl there.

Somebody put Sarah on my lap in the back seat. Heather was with me. Walter drove with Sheridan beside him. We flew into town, Walter admonishing me to breath into her mouth. I did, even though I didn't know the technique and I knew she was gone. She was so still, so heavy, so cold. She was wet and sandy, her hair, her eyes.

At the railroad tracks on Fifth Street a freight was shunting back and forth. Walter took a left, went around some construction, five extra blocks to cross the tracks, then five more back again. At the emergency door to the hospital, someone took Sarah out of my arms for the last time.

The head nurse argued that she should call Henry, not I. However, I prevailed, to my everlasting regret. Better it had been an impersonal messenger.

Louis Booth appeared and shoved us all out of the room whilst he tried open heart massage. Later I asked him why. "Because it was the only thing I could think might be helpful, even though I knew she was gone too long." Louis had brought Sarah into the world. She was three weeks overdue. Was she reluctant to arrive?

* * *

Sarah's drowning left us all wondering how we were going to make it through each day. It was natural to me, in the tradition of my family, to bring Sarah back to the ranch until her funeral. A day…a night…another half day. Sarah came in a white casket with white satin lining. She was clean and wearing her favorite dress, the same dress she had been wearing the morning she died. She'd had a little tea party with tiny cups and saucers, teapot, creamery, and sugar bowl. I had set this up at a little table on the lawn where she happily entertained imaginary guests.

Now Sarah's hair was dry and lay in natural waves. The funeral people even asked Fay Symons, who lived nearby and knew Sarah well, to see if her hair was right. It was, and she was as beautiful as she always had been. We put her on the closed porch where any and all could visit or not.

The children gathered around.

Sheridan: "She will never know pain or sickness."

Tyler: Not a word.

Heather: "Why, she is already with Jesus!"

Molly had been in South Dakota, but was soon home. She gasped and said, "She is so beautiful!"

Jamie, 18 months old, simply missed his constant companion.

Several days later I was washing dishes when Tyler told me that Sarah's death was not an accident. God took her because he needed her more than we did.

I said to Henry that we were lucky to have her for four years. "No," he said, "I wanted her for all my life, to know her growing up."

* * *

August 6, 1983

Just before dawn I cooked Henry's breakfast while he saddled and loaded his horse into the trailer. He and Sheridan and Sam Morton were going to move some cows and calves to another pasture with better water. For once I was able to go back to sleep. In an extremely deep slumber I was taking care of my beautiful girl child. She was four years old. I was protecting her from all danger, insisting to someone just out of my sight that I could do it. We laughed and played. Sometimes her features became old, not old-age, it seems, but old-wisdom, like she knew more than I, like she knew all there is to know.

Coming up from the depths to consciousness I had a rosy feeling, knowing that I had had a lovely visit with Sarah. I was wrong, of course, about my protecting her; however, the old-wisdom look was right, because even if she lived only for four years, she knew all there is to know.

Molly, Henry, Sarah, Tyler, Jamie, Mary, Heather and Sheridan, 1958

* * * * *

Bones

'Twas a beautiful early Saturday morning in April 1961, when Henry suggested we ride out to the calving pasture to see how many calves were born that night. While I was dressing, he saddled up the sorrel horse for me and rode him around the corral a bit, wondering if he would not be in too high a fettle for me to ride. His name was George and I was delighted to mount him, on my flat saddle.

The sun had risen brilliantly over the eastern hills. Henry spotted a calf with scours, and with throw-rope in hand galloped off to rope it and give it a bolus. George was eager to follow and started to canter, but I was not sure of him yet and drew up the reins. He did not buck, but in his disappointment merely kicked up his heels. Over his head I tumbled, like a fly flicked off his back.

Lying supine I looked at the blue, blue sky. Fleecy white clouds floated by.

I thought of the day in Normandy when I had scrambled over a hedgerow away from our camouflaged tents and foxholes and lay in an open field. It was warm and sunny that August day in 1944, and lying on my back I had looked at a blue, blue sky with fleecy white clouds floating placidly by. I had pondered: which is normal, which is real life: war or peace? Those thoughts filled my mind again. Then a soldier fleetingly crossed my mind. There were more soldiers, all of them infantrymen, and I longed to be one of them wearing a khaki uniform with a webbed belt that had a little kit hooked on it–morphine. I could take the morphine, then all this pain that seeped into my very bones would go away.

France…soldiers…morphine. Don't move. I returned to the sky when I heard galloping hooves and felt the ground vibrating under me. Then Henry was kneeling beside me. "Please roll me onto my side." He did so very gently then was gone. I was certain he was gone for hours, but I guess it was only ten or fifteen minutes before he returned with Sheridan. They sat me up, then helped me stand, then lay me in the back seat, on my side. What a bumpy road to town! Dear Louis was waiting at his office and came out to the car for a look. "Take her to the hospital."

There I was helped out of the car and walked to the stretcher. "Please put me on my side," say I. "Oh dear, many years ago after our 100 mile mountain ride I asked you, Henry, if I could please go back to a flat saddle. You said, 'Yes, but don't wear boots and britches around town.' And here I am embarrassing you at the hospital!"

Back on the stretcher after x-rays. Louis was holding my hand as we rolled down the corridor. "Mary, you have broken your right collarbone and scapula and three vertebrae just below your waist."

"But Louis, I can still go to the May Festival in Ann Arbor next Wednesday, can't I?"

Will I ever forget the answer of the ever gentle, fatherly Louis? "We'll see."

Returning from the shower one day to be rebound and put back to bed, I was confronted by Louis and an elderly gentleman. Soon I was standing there stark naked, the elderly gentleman taking all sorts of measurements of me. After all, he was the best saddle-maker in Wyoming—who better to make the metal-and-leather removable brace for my back? What a contraption! Over the shoulders, two straps across my chest which buckled in back—cinches you might say—contoured from shoulder to behind, all bound in white leather, with fancy yellow stitching on the cinches yet!

* * * * *

Jamie

August 1967. Jamie was nine years old and looking forward to leaving the country school for town school. Instead Louis took out his appendix. A few days later I took him back to Louis to remove his stitches. He removed one stitch. Yellow fluid appeared. Louis said we should take him to a specialist in Billings.

At St. Vincent's hospital two pediatricians and three surgeons met every morning to confer about Jamie. One said, "If he would just drink a milkshake that would help." All this time Jamie was going downhill. They put him in isolation. Jamie could eventually identify a nurse's footsteps and would tremble before she came in, because he knew it was going to be another shot. He had fifty-six shots in all. One of the hardest parts was the surgeon who came in every morning and talked about operating as he was leaning right over Jamie.

One day a surgeon came in and said, "We cannot wait any longer. We must operate immediately." Jamie was whisked away. I asked another doctor what had happened to Jamie." "How do I know, we didn't see him when he was first ill."

They found an abscess and put in a drain, and a few days later I took him home. He proceeded to lose more weight and to curl over on one side, and again his temperature shot up. Back to Billings twice, for two more operations.

From the hospital windows, we had watched a maple tree turn from summer green to brilliant red. We took him home after all the leaves had fallen, the day he said he would like a hamburger and a milkshake. After that year, Jamie was more aware of others' hurts. The experience was profound.

Mary and Jamie making butter, 1965

In late fall Jamie entered Highland Park, fifth grade. During his illness he had been tutored only in arithmetic. By Christmas he was well and I took him skiing with cousins in the Big Horn Mountains, at Antelope Butte.

Well into the skiing day I was told that Jamie was coming down in the basket. At the hospital, x-rays showed broken bones in his right leg. Louis set the breaks and Jamie was put to bed. The next morning when we arrived at the hospital, I glanced at his bed and looked out the window. Jamie said, "Well, didn't you see my legs?" I didn't want to. They were *both* in casts. I was told to get him a wheelchair that would elevate one leg.

After a three day hunt I found that rare treasure at a nursing home. Because Henry was busy as usual with the law, I'm the one who wheeled Jamie to the car, got him in and then put the wheelchair in, and at school got it out and got him into it. When the principal saw him, he exclaimed with envy, "Where did you find that wheelchair? May I borrow it when Jamie is finished with it?" He himself was in a wheelchair, having had a snowmobile accident.

A Burgess Christmas card

My Painting Life

My first art had been of my mouse, Sniffles. When I was expecting my first child, I made curtains for the baby room. They were a very fine voile and I used fabric paint to paint flowers on the hem. For years I did a lot of refinishing of furniture I would find at secondhand stores or auctions.

I was busy with babies and furniture and didn't think about painting until one Sunday in church my friend Bunny had in tow a silver-haired man wearing a red blazer, chinos, and tennis shoes—and back then people didn't dress like that in church. I asked her who he was. Rupert Conrad, a painter who traveled around the state on weekends, staying at someone's house, giving painting workshops. He happened to be staying at Bunny's house. I asked Sheridan, who already had paints, whether he would like to join Rupert's class. "Yes, I will if you will." We did.

It took me awhile to realize, in Rupert's painting class, that I'd spent a whole hour concentrating on what I was painting. It was the first hour I hadn't thought about Sarah since she had died almost two years earlier. At first I felt guilty, then I thought, "No, I don't have to feel guilty about not thinking about her." The beginning of a healing.

Sheridan and I went out to the back of the ranch and painted, working with oils. Sheridan did hills, a cowboy, and a few other things. Rupert was impressed with Sheridan and his hills. Between Saturdays I would ask Sheridan to paint with me. "Oh, Mom, painting is for a rainy day." I was the one who was hooked. Rupert lived in Casper, but was from Detroit and knew the Huron River well. He stayed with us often as he made his circuit.

I soon got involved with four ladies who loved to paint. We decided that we would go outdoors and paint on Thursdays. Dagmar was our leader, you might say. We were all into oils and we would paint at one of our homes. Because all four of us lived in the country, there was no end of scenery.

Painting in the country. Bunny in the foreground.

In the summer I was overwhelmed with cooking for farmhands and doing things with the children. One day Dagmar called and I said, "I just can't do it." But she said, "Drop those dishes and get over here right now. We're not having excuses." My niece Jennifer was with us and she said, "Go!" So I did, and the cares just melted away. Those Thursdays meant a great deal to all of us, beyond the painting. It was our "away day," and we all needed that refreshing time. We would paint in between so that we would have something to bring the following Thursday to be critiqued. That camaraderie makes you paint and keeps you in a rhythm.

Eventually Dagmar said, “Mary, the Wyoming Artists’ Association is meeting in Casper this year. Take a couple of your paintings.”

I said, “I couldn’t possibly—and show people.”

“Yes, you can. Then you’ll find they aren’t so bad.”

I did hang my paintings, and they weren’t so bad. So for years a group of us would go to the Wyoming Artists’ Association, which was held in various towns around the state. We became acquainted with many artists. Bunny was president one year, so the meeting was held in Sheridan. I too became president and held the meeting in Sheridan. I was the first to have artists bring their equipment and work during the days of the meeting and receive critiques. They’ve been doing that ever since.

I worked backwards from oils to drawing with a pen to drawing with a pencil and eventually, bravely, to watercolors. It was a Famous Artists Course that made me use watercolors. A beautiful sheet of watercolor paper is harder to face than a canvas.

I went out to Dayton, twenty-five miles away in the foothills of the Big Horn Mountains, to paint a white church. I was experimenting with the idea of having a soft orange underlay. No one was around, but eventually a man came by and looked at my painting for the longest time. He finally said, "I don't know what you're doing, but I was married in that church, and that isn't what it looks like."

There was a quaint church in Sheridan that I thought would be fun to paint. But to get far enough from it, I had to be across the street in someone's yard. I rang the doorbell of the residence and asked a man whether I could paint the church. For a long time he looked at it and at me. Then he asked, "What color?"

I wanted to paint a silo and the infinity of the railroad tracks near Wyarno. I set up in the middle of the railroad tracks. Just as I finished and walked off the tracks, a train rolled through. I had not heard a sound.

One of my favorite stories from a show concerns Henry, who was very well known in the state, having been a State Senator. He was introduced to a lady who said, "Henry Burgess? Oh, the husband of the painter, Mary Burgess." He used to laugh over that.

I Went to the Denver Stock Show

Jamie

The Pony Track Ranch

Alice Fuller was the wife of Bud Fuller, one of Henry's best friends from first grade on. Alice and Bud were ranchers also. When Alice and I collaborated on paintings, she might get the bare bones idea for a painting and then we'd both paint it. Always acrylic on unprimed canvas. They were marvelous. So large, we had to paint them on the floor. Sometimes she'd say, "Mary, your arms are longer than mine, so you do the center part."

A collaboration with Alice Fuller

Any time you have a show you have to do the some of the hardest work of an artist: ensure that all the paintings are signed, titled, framed, and priced. Then declare yourself and your philosophy. Here are some of my declarations:

These abstract collaborations with Alice Fuller have opened a new field of working design and color and form. To paint intuitively and in concert with one another is an adventure in trust and respect for one another's abilities, audacity and personal proclivities. Actually, it has been a test of maturity. People who have viewed our works in progress always say, 'Well, you are having fun.' It is mid-afternoon and we stare at each other numb with fatigue for leaning, squatting, crawling or leaning over the canvas as it lays flat on the floor. (We are not into drips.) Fatigue also because since nine in the morning we have been decision-making every step of the way. Oh yes, we, too, would say we are having fun.

On a collection of paintings:

The challenge of design and color leads me further into abstraction. This series addresses the problem of dividing a surface into three shapes as simply as possible and making them work.

On Sumi-e:

Oriental brush painting emboldens individuality. Each brush stroke must count because there is no turning back. Freedom demands the greatest discipline. It is an intellectual pursuit. It is control of manipulating one's brush. It should reflect work in any other media. It is exercising the use of negative space and makes the most of black to white.

For a gallery in Sheridan:

As one friend of hers often comments, "Mary Burgess walks where angels fear to tread." This is true of Mary as an individual as well as an artist. Her life is unique and constantly moving, and her paintings reflect this pattern of uncommon and kinetic experience. Since she began painting over ten years ago, she has devoted as much time to her art as being ranch-hand and family woman will allow. She can be found sketching behind the wheel of a barley trick, collecting collage and subject material on a cattle drive, or contemplating her brush stroke while stirring a pot of borscht. The long hours spent in the hills while moving cattle have given her ample opportunity for studying the hues, shapes and feelings which she has transferred to her multi-faceted paintings. Some even refer to her work as 'mystic.'

My painting friends and I all attended various workshops given by noted artists, gleaning something from every one. One of the most valuable lessons, taught by Rupert: "Draw with a pen. Don't use an eraser."

Rupert said to pick a favorite artist and copy him if you like, but then you have to put him away and become your own person; yet you will have picked up what you like about that painter.

At one point I picked Jackson Pollack with an aim to see what would happen when I applied different layers of paint without a brush on a large canvas. I learned that, just as in handwriting, one cannot copy another person's gestures. You can't forge; at least, I couldn't. As soon as I say this I realize how many people accurately copy another's style. That's pure forgery. They may be very talented; they have to be. What I really wanted to do after that painting was a series of ten and see where I came out at the end, how different my gestures and colors would be. Never got that far.

Painting is a shortcut to knowing people very well, in that no matter what we're painting, we reveal much of ourselves. This is true of all the people we met throughout Wyoming. Bunny and I were in a bridge club together for years before we started painting. And it was only then that we really became more than acquaintances. Working together forms strong bonds.

Once one centers painting on abstraction it can be very hard to go back to painting a barn, because abstraction is an ultimate adventure. Going down unknown paths or letting it lead you into unknown realms of introspection, perhaps. You never know what's going to happen next. It is an adventure in design and color and making a painting work at least two or three ways. It is hard work.

Several of us took lessons from Richard Martinson, an art teacher at Sheridan College. Design, three dimensions, gestures, drawing. There were two classes a week, three hours each. The classes kept us in the rhythm of painting, regardless of what was going on in our lives. He was an excellent teacher and invaluable to many students.

I took first place for an oil portrait at some show in Wyoming. When I got it back with its little ribbon I sat down and showed Henry. "How do you like this painting?" I asked. "I like any of your paintings; they keep you happy on the ranch." However, the more we traveled and I insisted that we go to art museums the more Henry understood my art.

I did not paint for about three months. Molly caught me with my brushes one day. "Mother, I'm so glad you are painting again."

"I didn't know you liked my paintings."

"I don't like many, but you are a nicer mother when you paint."

Well, I think it was that I had my own thing to do that they appreciated. I would come home more exuberant and interested in them and the world when I'd been painting. And I always ate like a football player after I'd been painting.

There was a gentle man, an artist, who lived near Birney, Montana. His name was Jim Ryan. He visited our ranch a few times. When Jamie was just a little fellow, Jim died on the porch of the Sheridan Inn of a heart attack. Sometime after that Jamie and I were in the utility room at the ranch. There was a tack on the floor and I was barefoot. Jamie said, "Oh, no, no, Mother, don't walk in here. It will kill you. You know, like that artist Jim Ryan who died of a tack."

Several raw stumps of trees at the Pony Track yearned for my brush. I started from the eye of the tree.

I have used many places to paint. The first was a corner of the living room at the ranch. Then, between the barn and the shed there were two rooms. One was used as a smoke room, and the other side was a small garage. We put a big window in the garage side, and added a little heater. It had an earthen floor and I painted out there for several years. I was trying to give up smoking and declared to my family that I would, but I found that if I went out there to do a little painting after supper I could have a cigarette or two. Heather caught me: "I thought maybe you were smoking out here!"

Another time, I'd gone out in my nightie in the middle of the night with an urge to paint. Molly was brought home by her date and they came over to the studio and we chatted for a minute and later Molly's date said, "Does your mother always paint in the middle of the night in her nightie?"

Between the house and what we called the cottage was another little building, the creamery. Our ranch had been at one time a dairy. I set up my studio in there. Cold in the winter, hot in the summer, and no room.

Sheridan, Tyler, and Molly all had their bedrooms in the cottage. The fourth bedroom was kind of a guest room. I took it over as a studio. I had been accumulating more equipment, more paints, more canvases.

As Sheridan and Molly moved on, I took over two rooms in the back of the cottage. I wanted to make it into one room. Henry said, "Oh, no. It's too much work and it would be too expensive to make it into one room." Bertie came out the next morning and I told her of Henry's decision. She said, with a twinkle in her eye, "Don't you have a crowbar? Don't you have a saw? Don't you have a...?" So we spent the day tearing down the closets that separated these two rooms.

We were apprehensive when Henry walked in and took a look. His smile was broad as he said, "I might have known you two would do this. You've done a wonderful job. The only thing is you've taken down the part that supports the ceiling." And then we had to have a professional come in and put in a supporting beam. Yes, it did become a refuge. No telephone in the cottage. And I spent many happy hours, months, and years in that room.

The mighty painter, painting bookshelves at the Pony Track Ranch, overturned the ladder with a shelf for the paint pot, with said paint pot still there.

Ranch Stories

That little creek we live on, Lower Prairie Dog, overwhelmed itself a couple of weeks ago. We had a full-fledged flood. The house is about twenty feet above and we knew the water would not get to it. Nonetheless, the excitement of watching rising water was intense. The corrals, the land beyond the creek where we park our equipment, and the road to the bridge were all three feet deep with running water. Awesome. The whole Sheridan area and many other communities were on a high. Voices loud, bodies tensed, some homes evacuated.

A couple of days later, exhaustion set in. But, oh, are we green! And every reservoir is filled to overflowing. Then we gathered cattle on the hills for branding and we discovered many large and small mudslides. The horses picked their footing carefully. Dewy grasses, sagebrush, and wild flowers sparkled in the rising sun.

Mary riding on the hills of The Divide

Later Henry wanted to salt some cattle on The Divide only to discover that a washout on Dutch Creek, the one that also flows through Sheridan's place, took out his bridge. We found a dam gone and the support for an irrigating flume caught in the old dam. As Henry's geologist brother says, "Floods are society's problem, not nature's." Agreed. We simply watched nature going about her business.

We found a lone antelope running hard. She was leading us away from her baby. Three great blue herons rose from the creek bottom. One beaver dam is gone, three others intact. Five foot-long snapping turtles lazed near the beaver ponds. The meadowlarks sang and the prairie dogs chattered. If there were red foxes, coyotes, porcupines, skunks, or rattlesnakes around we didn't see them. The wild flowers were rampant and brilliant.

"The Three Bulls." That's what Henry's brother, who took this picture, called it.

Down the creek a ways lived a widow. In 1974, while making her usual rounds checking the calving heifers, she found one in trouble. The heifer was lying down in the sagebrush, calf halfway out and alive, but appearing to be hiplocked. The rancher went quickly to her house for supplies and to summon help from her nearest neighbor. When they returned, the heifer no longer had her calf, but she was really hurting. They managed her into the pickup and took her to the corral for antibiotics, food, and water. About four feet from where the helpless young cow had lain were the remains of her newborn. Coyotes had come and stolen the calf right out of its mother, then devoured whatever they took to be edible of the little critter.

* * *

In 1983 we had a couple of Navajos, Herman and Andy, in the bunkhouse for fencing and irrigating and odd jobs. They cooked for themselves, made their own tortillas and biscuits, and could do just about everything. We got used to their broad faces and their walks and talks. I saw them daily, but they kept to themselves. The bunkhouse remained spotless with beds perfectly made. I can't describe the incredible mess plain old American boys usually kept it in.

Before Herman and Andy, we had Mexicans who also cooked for themselves and kept the bunkhouse spotless. I know this because I often took over desserts.

Outbuildings at the ranch. The bunkhouse is in the foreground.

One day Herman was irrigating the meadow. The Sheriff's men, rounding up illegal Mexican immigrants, came right up to him and were going to put him in the cage on the back of their pickup.

Herman said, "You can't touch me. I am FBI."

"What?"

"Full Blooded Indian!"

How he chuckled. But I still had to get him out of jail for being drunk and disorderly when he went to town.

* * *

Moorcroft, Wyoming – 1984

Moorcroft lies east of Gillette and somewhat west of Sundance and Devil's Tower. The town has grown to a population of 1,500. Our steers summer just north of here off the D Road. The land is high prairie country, softly rolling hills, good grass and plenty of sagebrush with good watering holes on Miller Creek. This particular spot is in the path of the old longhorn cattle drives from Texas to Miles City, Montana.

On this day I expected to join Henry, Jamie, and Rusty Hollar and his gang in gathering our steers to ship them to Torrington for auction. It snowed during the night and whilst the town itself seemed mild, that spot just north is windswept and bitter cold. I'm sure that is not always true; however, the weather seems to know when the Burgesses are coming. It did not take much urging from the guys for me to head back to town after taking them and their horses by trailer to the farthest end of the pasture.

I went to the drugstore of Moorcroft and discovered a soda fountain. The front is ceramic tile with an interesting motif. The spinning stools are chrome and orange. There is carbonated water to make the sodas. Despite the cold I found myself indulging in a vanilla soda! More to my amazement, I was told this is one of only a few soda fountains left in Wyoming. Torrington, Chugwater, and Buffalo share the honor. This one is sixty years old.

* * *

An Easterner was visiting the ranch. Come Sunday I thought I might show him that I did not always wear blue jeans and that my legs aren't bad. I donned a short, narrow skirt, a blouse, stockings and high-heeled pumps. We had not yet heard of panty hose so I was properly trussed in a girdle and stockings. I looked for the men and found them in the corral. Henry had a heifer down that needed a little help calving. He yelled, "Get over here and sit on her head." I looked at the Easterner and he looked at me, aghast.

"Who me?"

"Yes, you."

So I daintily perched on her head, knees together, heels digging into corral dirt and tugging down my skirt as best I could.

It was a gentle pull and the calf was fine. I thanked the easterner for helping me up. By the time they came in for Sunday dinner I was back in my jeans.

* * *

At the ranch, as at most ranches, the land and the sky and the doing of the weather are immediate. There are enormous cottonwoods and silver leaf poplars in the front yard, a narrow porch sheltering the south-facing front of the house, and an old white fence, with railroad ties for the posts, at the edge of the lawn. Several ranch meadows come right up to the white fence. When August turned into September and the rains did not come, the dust was thick in the air under the hot and relentless blue sky. When the sun was lowering, the dust turned the world into spun gold.

Wintertime always presents a challenge under that same blue sky with the sun brilliant on the white snow, the temperature often at ten or twenty or thirty or even forty below. The hay equipment, tractors, and cars refuse to start in spite of heater hookups. Summer heats up to over 100 degrees, but how can we complain of our heat? We cool down at night and there is always a brief freshness in the early morn.

In between the temperature extremes are other extremes, soft and sunny days. And rains to fill the reservoirs and help the grass and the grains grow. Then there are the rains turned to floods as the banks of Lower Prairie Dog and Dutch Creeks fill beyond their limits. For miles up and down these creeks often the only crossing that holds is Harris Crossing, so named for the young man who, while visiting Molly, was put to work by Henry. Henry could not abide a visitor just doing nothing during the days, so Harris was put to work staking old tires along the edge of the crossing.

Hoppers are finicky, leaving every weed to flourish. I have threatened to make grasshopper soup just from those on our front porch and several in the house.

* * *

Eighty acres in front of the house are in four strains of corn for silage. It is the first corn off this ranch, which sent Jamie scouring Nebraska, Wyoming, and Montana for a secondhand corn chopper and cultivator, which we purchased. Jamie and Joe, who was in Jamie's high school class, have put them back into first class condition. Yesterday Jamie gave me a tour on the four-wheeler buggy to the other side of the eighty acres of corn and I followed him on foot between the cornrows. Cool, shady, non-prickly leaves brushed against us. Tassels topping, some of which are as tall as six-foot-four Jamie. The actual corn is yet to come. However, we are not the only ones in anticipation. Coons inspect every night. The deer will take their share, and perhaps the wild turkeys will show up for the feast also.

* * *

Polo season started yesterday. Sheridan played superbly, and so did his horses. There are four avid polo players here from the East looking for horses. They met Sheridan in a local Big Horn bar afterwards wanting to purchase four horses. He slept on it and made his decision this morning: that in spite of the vast amount of money offered and that he would be completely impoverished for the season, he will keep his horses. We applaud his decision. He is proud, however, because he raised and trained these thoroughbreds himself. Besides, they are good cow ponies.

* * *

Our first spring, Henry took me and two cups of coffee into the living room, telling the children to stay out. I was pleased we were going to have a tête-à-tête.

He asked, "Wouldn't you like a dishwasher?"

"Oh, I'd like that very much."

"During haying season we will need extra help. They can stay in the bunkhouse but will need to be fed."

"Oh? How long is the haying season?"

"About a month for the first cutting. Then the men will be gone until the second cutting, another month, in August."

"Where do we get this help?"

"I'll go to the Job Service."

The summer invasion lasted for over thirty years. They came late June and stayed until the last hay was up, which was sometime after Labor Day. There were three to five every summer. Eat with us they did. Three meals a day, Sundays too, relentlessly.

Hands from the Job Service:

A man with graying hair and piercing blue eyes—except for a couple of missing teeth he was the picture of a Senator. Actually, he was a beachcomber from Hawaii who liked to put up loose hay, which we did the first years.

An absolutely hairless man. I asked one of the other hands if he was hairless everywhere. "Yes, everywhere." Molly didn't want to sit next to him because he smelled. We put him next to me because I couldn't smell him but couldn't stand to look at him.

John, who was a pretty good hand, stayed into the fall when we needed more help. I was to pick Henry up at the airport at nine p.m. and asked John if he wanted to go to town. He did, so I dropped him off where I should pick him up. Henry didn't arrive; it was cold; I picked John up and started back to the ranch. John said, "Mrs. Burgess, a policeman behind us wants you to stop." The officer came over to my side and shined his flashlight on my driver's license and then at John, who turned his face away. He said, "You just went through a stop sign. Don't do it again." When he got back to his car, I said, "I don't like what he's thinking," and stopped him as he started to drive away. "Henry was not on the plane. This is just a hired man. I'm taking him back to the ranch." He said, "Don't worry Mrs. Burgess, I see a lot of things, and I don't talk." We drove back to the ranch in silence.

One day John was sent to town to get a part. He did not return. That evening, the Sheriff called and said John had been forging checks all over town and had taken a cab, wearing only his jean jacket, up to Billings, Montana. The cab driver was suspicious and called the police on his radio. The Sheriff's men picked John up before he reached Billings. He was on the Most Wanted list for having stolen cars around the country. He ended up in the Montana State Penitentiary.

We had many fine boys from the East Coast and from Sheridan. Boynton Glidden came, son of a Harvard classmate of Henry's. Only fifteen, he toughed out the long hot days of haying and returned the next summer. His younger brother and sister came out, in time. Eventually our three daughters joined the crew, rotating two in the fields and one in the house helping me. Naively, I followed Henry's plan and washed all those dirty clothes in our machine. Elizabeth's daughters came out, one by one. I called them my scullery maids. Jennifer, Mary, and Betsy—I could not have done without them.

Friends and families and their friends visited from around the world. Enriching summers for all of us.

After my broken bones, Molly, fifteen years old, cooked and managed three meals all summer long. Henry had the boys haying on Sundays too. The reward was time off to go fishing at Kearny Lake, in the mountains. In autumn and spring Molly, Tyler, Heather, and Sheridan were often out of bed by four or five to help work cattle, trailing them to summer or winter pastures. Tyler was our true cowgirl.

We invited a seasoned ranch couple for dinner. Greg, who had a hesitation in his speech, looked me in the eye and said, "Mary, you have the most beautiful...." As he hesitated I wondered: eyes? hair? face? No. "Haystacks!" Loose hay it was.

Vignettes

Regarding Tattoos

In the Philippines we saw sailors who had tattoos. The Igorots, the mountain people in Northern Luzon, were divided into five tribes and each tribe had identifying tattoos on their faces and arms. At one point I longed to be a boy, so that I could become a sailor and get a tattoo. That longing fell away as I became more of a woman. But it was still in the back of my mind to have a tattoo.

Eventually, in Denver with Henry, I went to Rex's Tattoo Parlor. He made a sketch of a flower for the inside of my right wrist. I said, "Okay." He proceeded to tattoo the flower and then he said, "Now, should we make it a red flower with green leaves?" I said, "No, I don't think I can wake up to that. I don't think Henry can wake up to that."

It took me two years to realize that the pain running down my two outside fingers was not arthritis. It was caused by the self-consciousness of my hand. What I had not counted on was that my right hand is the one with which I gesticulate. Therefore, I unwittingly was showing it much of the time.

Many a morning Henry would wake up laughing because there would be my tattoo. He said, "You can get a tattoo anywhere else, too." I couldn't see much point in that.

When I was in the hospital for a week with an IV, it was very difficult to expose my wrist, but no nurse ever said a word. However, a couple of weeks later I was in the grocery store and one of the employees there smiled broadly and said, "I hear you have a tattoo." I said, "Now how come you know?" He said, "My wife is a nurse." We were in one long aisle and he looked all the way around and then showed me his tattoo on his upper arm.

Another friend came smiling up to me and said, "I hear you have a tattoo. When I was kind of high in high school I got a tattoo on my wrist, too." A third man was a stockbroker. He was intrigued with my tattoo and because of it was convinced I would want to read three books of sailing between England and Cape Hope in the nineteenth century. I read all three books. They were delightful.

At a dinner party I was sitting opposite an orthopedic surgeon. I had seen him a couple of times because of a growth on the top of my finger. As usual I was gesticulating with my right hand and his mouth dropped open and he said, "What is that?" I said, "It's what you think it is: a tattoo." "You mean to tell me I've seen you and didn't even notice it?"

It is interesting that the strongest reactions have come from men. Women have just said, "Oh, Mary, how could you?" I've never regretted it.

* * * * *

Madame Arcati, 1983

In January, I prepared panels for a large series of small oils, to be simple local landscapes. But the few I did inevitably turned into flowers and color studies in abstract. Then I got sidetracked. I was very firmly encouraged to audition for the Civic Theater Guild's *Noel Coward Review*—a half hour of *Private Lives*, a half hour of Blythe Spirit, and a sprinkling of his songs. I turned into Madame Arcati, who leaves her bike off stage and wears basketball shoes dyed in tea, a sort of suit, and long beads. Madame Arcati lives in a world of her own and conducts a séance after doing her own dance steps to "Always."

It was hard to gauge how much I had learned in a few weeks of theater. Despite having always been enchanted by the theater, I never really considered being on the stage myself, and it was a revelation. In the past, thanks to Mother and Daddy, going to the theater was always a delightful experience. The Lydia Mendelssohn summer stock in Ann Arbor was a childhood habit. Jane Cowl in *Twelfth Night* for instance. Occasional matinees in Detroit, notably Gilbert and Sullivan's *The Mikado*. A few on Broadway. And theatricals abounded in England during the war. There were valiant performances offered by the USO to troops, plays at University High in Ann Arbor and at Brent School in the Philippines, and operas and ballets in Paris.

But on the stage of our little ninety seat Carriage House Theater in Sheridan, I made my true debut. I thought our director, Lynne Simpson, was colorblind when she told us to wait in the green room, which is clearly brick, blue, and red. I was taken aback by the suggestion that I should break a leg. How could we manage rehearsals with the pounding of nails and the sawing of wood going on? And I was dumbfounded during a lovely rehearsal solo in progress when two young women were asked to step upon the stage in full light. For a police line up? No. To determine which makeup base the director preferred.

Because this was a musical review we had a fine musical director as well. Kit Johnson spent most of his time in the doldrums over our mostly amateur voices—a motley group by age and inclination, selected by whatever means amateur theater comes into being. However, he remained diligent and patient, and through his own tremendous talent as teacher and musician made the chorus cohesive. The soloists stood on their own. For my part, I sang as softly as possible, hoping no one heard me at all and that I didn't blurt out during the rests. On high notes I merely mouthed the words and smiled.

During the séance I had to faint and fall to the floor with my beautifully clad feet resting upright on my stool. My stockings and knee length panties kept me decently indecent. Then I got to change into charming pink and gray to sing with the chorus.

We performed eight times, all sell-outs. The set and costumes were superb. Great fun.

* * * * *

Town Adventures

As I was going to town one day dressed in my favorite gray velveteen dress, white gloves and high heels, I realized I must stop by our antiquated tank to fill-er-up. Then I hopped out of the car to open a gate in the barnyard, then hopped into the car to drive over, then hopped out again to close the gate. At the top of the lane I turned left onto Lower Prairie Dog Creek Road, at last headed for a ladies' tea in town. The road was being widened and rebuilt at the bend. It had rained heavily the night before and our heavy non-power-steering station wagon sank up to its hubs.

Now this road is not much traveled, so I said to myself, "I might as well start walking." I put my white gloves in my purse, and, carrying my shoes, I daintily stepped out and mired down in mud more than ankle-deep, holding up my mid length gray velveteen dress. After a few plodding steps, I stopped to laugh at the picture

I made, and actually the deep mud felt good. I also thought once more of what I had vowed to myself as we plodded through Belgian and Dutch mud during World War II: that I was never going to live anywhere there was mud. I would be a city girl wearing satin and lace. At last an old friend and fellow rancher came by to laugh with me and take me to town.

* * *

As I was going to town one day I met the Queen going the other way. It's true. Queen Elizabeth of England had just taken a tour of Main Street, Sheridan,Wyoming, and she and her entourage were returning to the Wallop Ranch near Big Horn, where she was a guest of Jean Wallop. As the first police car with lights blazing passed little ol' me in the big blue Suburban, I waved madly. It seemed like they all waved back.

Henry and I had already invited members of her flight crew to visit our ranch. On the Sunday morning whilst I was cooking, Henry picked up four mufti-clad gentlemen at the Holiday Inn. He took them up Dutch Creek to The Divide for a good look at our Hereford cattle and Thoroughbred horses, some deer, antelope, and a porcupine or two. Up close was sagebrush, tiny wildflowers, good grass, a prairie dog town. The land itself is contoured by ridges and deep draws which cosseted juniper. In the distance, about twenty miles or so, rise the beautiful Big Horn Mountains, with Montana to the north and endless hills to the south.

On the ridges of The Divide, the dirt roads edge along deadly drop-off ridges. During Sunday dinner at the Pony Track I was aghast to discover that our guests consisted of both of the Queen's pilots and her navigator! But then, Henry is a safe driver.

* * * * *

An Encounter with Fame, 1983

A screen and TV writer had been in touch with Henry for months wanting to tape Henry's history from 1941 through the Los Baños raid in the Philippines. Finally, Henry set aside a Thursday and Friday at home. Dan Gordon, the writer, said a producer was coming with him. Then the night they arrived he called to say they were at The Sheridan Center and a wife had come too. I asked Henry about meals. He said, "Let's see what they are like first." Henry brought them out at ten a.m., and at first I thought the producer was a woman with gorgeous locks of silver. But physique in sweatshirt, Levi's, and boots, plus voice, proved him a most attractive man with a petite blonde, exotically dressed wife.

The only preamble was this producer asking Henry if he knew what kind of work he did. Henry said, "No." The producer only proclaimed his mission to be upbeat, positive, "it may sound corny", but patriotic messages. So, Henry started taping. Two hours without a break and I thought I'd better get something on the kitchen table. Peanut butter sandwiches. During lunch the producer kept telling stories about the problems of being a celebrity. We were most attentive and empathetic, all the time wondering, "Who on earth is he?" The taping continued, seven hours in all. Like the Ancient Mariner, Henry had to tell it all. His voice became almost a whisper, tears never far away. He was emotionally spent and once again somewhat cleansed.

We took them for a ride on The Divide behind our house. The producer kept commenting how it reminded him of the country for the "Little House on the Prairie." Michael Landon! His "celebrity problem" led us to introduce him to no one, not even to our children, except Jamie who happened to be there. Nor did we know the town was on its ear simply because he had arrived in Sheridan, and his identity had been discovered when he rented a car. When Henry was asked if he had met with Landon, he would say, "Well, if he won't tell, neither will I."

That project never got on the road. Mr. Landon became ill and died.

* * * * *

My Wayward Heart

My heart and I have been on many a wayward adventure. I consider myself to be a healthy individual, despite many ups and downs and hospital stays. All ills have been mended. Broken bones; chronic backaches; three ovarian cysts, one of which broke while making love, for heavens sake.

I've had six beautiful, healthy babies, each with two ears. By treading carefully our last was born early and well. I nursed them all. I started to smoke seriously when twenty-two years old serving in England in the American Red Cross. I left the war two and a half years later as a dedicated smoker and coffee and tea drinker. Drinks of the harder sort were merely social.

Marrying Henry did make my heart flip, but in the nature of a valentine. My heart adventures started just after mending all those broken bones which occurred when a horse and I parted company. With time on my hands and lots of pain killers (by shot—a very peppered bottom), I went up to two packs of delicious Camels a day, with tea or coffee or a drink. A package of cigarettes had hit an all time high, thirty cents. Occasionally, and always early in the morning, my heart would beat in high gear, but it returned to normal so quickly I ignored it for some time. Eventually I mentioned it to Louis Booth, but he never caught it out of rhythm. At this time in our lives we were attending many fabulous dinners and dancing parties. I had learned to drink bourbon and Coca-Cola before dinner and sip only Coke after. No hangover. Dr. Booth later remarked I probably would have been better off drinking whiskey after dinner rather than the Coke stimulant. In any event my morning episodes often correlated to night-before parties. They didn't necessarily have to be dances.

One day when my heart was racing, Dr. Booth rushed to the ranch to listen to it. Ah, yes indeed. My heart received a name, a title: Paroxysmal Atrial Tachycardia. Like a faucet, it is either on or off. The beat could even get up to two hundred, but no, this is not life threatening. Then started years of drugs, many experimental, to calm my increasing faucet beats. Hard for my family. Hard for my friends. Sometimes I simply blacked out and would fall in my tracks. Embarrassing. Only once did I have to get my head stitched up.

Also, I, who had always slept like a baby, was now wide awake two or three hours in the middle of the night. So by the time I was supposed to rise and shine to get the childrens' breakfasts, make their lunches for the one room country school, and see them off walking the almost mile lane, or taking them when too cold or rainy, my body was spent. Always a much too rude awakening from the deepest of sleeps attained just before dawn. And I'd be furious with Henry for waking me and then promptly leaving for the office. Often my heart's faucet would turn on in those relentless early morns. It took to a will of its own and for years would surprise me anytime, anywhere.

I am convinced the various drugs are mood altering. Depression and suicidal thoughts, and I learned much later that the children often assumed I was mad at them. Well, sometimes I was! I had visited with a cardiologist in Casper. He did not catch me out of rhythm, but he gave me strict orders: no nicotine, no caffeine, no stress, no fatigue. With a house full of teenagers? He ordered a different calmer-downer. Eventually I climbed over that incredibly high, thick cement wall and followed his first two orders. I usually take a nap, but the stress is part of life itself.

One day I defiantly cut back my medications and felt better and had no trouble. But a checkup with the doc, a young internist, revealed a steady irregular beat, so my heart changed titles to atrial fibrillation. He ordered me into the hospital immediately to receive five days and nights worth of blood thinner to prevent a possible stroke or death by blood clot, which could form during the pause in a beat.

I was playing lots of tennis, my lifelong favorite game. By this time, doubles only. I had a wonderful partner and we joined in the city competition one summer. I found that when I left the court I dragged to the car, and often wept with weakness on the way home and would spend the rest of the day in bed.

Henry and I went to New York on business. While Henry was busy I prowled the shops and galleries. Went to the Metropolitan Museum. Saw the kiosk to buy a ticket to the famous Van Gogh Show. But I didn't buy a ticket and didn't go to the show. I just needed a cup of tea. I dragged myself across the street to the Stanhope Hotel and bought a cup, with assorted cookies for $15.00. I perked up and walked back to our hotel.

I should have known something was really wrong when I wouldn't go to Van Gogh.

* * *

The Irma Hotel — Cody, Wyoming, 1987

Buffalo Bill built The Irma Hotel and named it for his daughter. Henry and Bob Wyatt, another attorney, were headed for the county court, and I tagged along. It is a beautiful drive over the Big Horns and I like to prowl Cody and look up friends. To humor me we engaged rooms on the second floor of The Irma, refurbished in the quaint style of Buffalo Bill's day.

Henry was long gone when I awoke that first morning. As I got up to dress I had a fleeting feeling that I was too tired to do anything, but I wanted to see a friend before looking into the courtroom, where the case would commence at nine thirty. While visiting, I became so tired I simply got into the Suburban and drove back to the hotel. Parked on the diagonal in front, rather than on the restaurant side where people usually enter.

Nobody was around as I lay my head on the newel post, contemplating the stairs to the second floor. On the post at the landing I lowered my head once more to study the remaining steps, and when they were accomplished I gratefully clung to the last post. I found myself staring into room 36, the door ajar. Bob Wyatt was sitting at a table in the back of the room, full face towards me, but his eyes were lowered, concentrating upon his writing. Looking at my watch—a couple of minutes past nine—I knew he was headed to the courtroom. No, no, I must not disturb him, so I silently made my way around the corner to room 20 and headed for the bed. Taking stock of myself, I felt a tremendous weariness, though no hurting anywhere nor shortness of breath. I was receding, going away, backing out—and terribly alone.

The phone was not within reach and whom should I call? I managed to get up to search for the maids, went down the hall gripping the high wainscoting, and thought of Mother who would have said I was dawdling. I heard the maids, but they were down the hall and around another corner. Too far, much too far. I once again retreated to room 20 and the bed, leaving the door wide open should someone chance by.

I thought of my dear friend Mops. She had called her daughter-in-law saying she did not feel well and to please cancel her hair appointment. That was a signal, and Sharon came to Mops immediately. I knew that I did not have what Mops had, but I had to be responsible and make a signal. I thought of Dean Sage who told his wife that he was very tired and took a nap from which he never awoke.

We had known Douglas Carr's family long before he was born and he was now a doctor of Internal Medicine in Cody. Keeping my head low I got to the bottom of the bed, grabbed the telephone cord and pulled it and the book to the bed and called his office. When the receptionist answered, I simply burst into tears. She asked for my name, location and room number. She told me to hang up and keep my head low. It never occurred to me to call 911; I wasn't *that* sick.

In a trice I heard bounding footsteps in the hall and three (I think) policemen appeared at my side. Of course my first thought was, "What have I done?" Then there were men in white and an oxygen line was put to my nose and I breathed deeply with relief.

They asked questions, took pulse and blood pressure, prowled in my purse for information on medications and retrieved same from the ledge and bawled me out, nicely, for putting different pills in one container. “No, I have no chest pain, no shortness of breath. No, you can’t hook the oxygen tube over my right ear because I haven’t one. No, don’t call my husband. What is my pulse?” Answer: it has gone *up* to twenty beats per minute.

They taped the tube to my cheek and said I was going to be sat up and moved to their sling-like chair. I sat up only to be gently pushed back. “You are not going to do anything. We are.” In the midst of this, The Irma’s manager was at the foot of the bed assuring me that all would be safe in room 20. One of those maids popped in, threw up her hands and fled. She was wearing pink.

The once deserted lobby was full of hovering faces as my chair became flat and I was moved to a proper stretcher. Oh, wretched me, shorn of self-control and dignity as helpless tears flowed down my temples. Wheeling through the door, I was freshly alarmed at the sight of whirling lights atop an ambulance parked in the middle of the street. For *me*? On board I was relieved to find windows in the doors. My only comment, I hope, was that this was different than viewing such a scene on TV.

West Park Hospital emergency room. The trauma of full attack by the life saving—life giving?—crew. The competent, elegant Doctor Douglas Carr. Plopped into the Intensive Care Unit. Doug said he would send a note to the courtroom for Henry to come right over. “Why don’t you just send him a note to call you?” He did, and Henry received it and slipped it into his pocket. After lunch at The Irma he looked at the note again and speculated that it might not be a social one at all. He came for a visit, then returned to court.

With all the care in the world, I still complained. How could I rest with a jackhammer at work under my bed? “It’s not under your bed, it’s under your floor. We are getting a new entrance.” The entrance was delayed during my twenty-four hours in Intensive Care, after which I was moved to the third floor with a heart monitor.

This was no heart attack. My strong and healthy little heart received a new title: Tachy-Brady Syndrome, a final disintegration of the electrical impulses which regulate heart beats. "Tachy"—the pulse goes up. "Brady"—it goes down. Brady had gone down and Tachy almost forgot to come back up.

"Doug, I am suppose to give a book review next Tuesday. Should I give it up?"

"No, keep working on it."

"Doug, do you think I need a pacemaker?" Not being my home doctor he was cautious but definite. "Yes, that's a good idea. Sometime in the spring."

Tyler drove over from Billings for a lovely visit. Sheridan offered to fly over to take me home. "Oh, no," says Doug, "I don't want you in a plane." The third floor of West Park Hospital in Cody was light and airy, with a caring and competent staff. Restful. I worked on my book review, the fascinating saga of Doctor Seymour Gray's experiences, *Beyond the Veil*, in Saudi Arabia.

That Saturday when Henry, Bob, and I reached the fine air on top of the Big Horns at the Antelope Butte Ski area we paused for a delicious lunch. I exclaimed to Henry, "But it is spring already!"

A consultation on Sunday, then tuck in the pacemaker on Wednesday. Me: "But I want this to be hush-hush, so that when I give my review on Tuesday the ladies might listen to my tale instead of wondering if or when I will drop."

Early Wednesday morning in Memorial Hospital of Sheridan County with Doctor Gould:

"What is the procedure?"

"Well, first I will make an incision, then muck out a pocket for the gadget. By the way, any reason you might want it on the left side rather than the right?"

"I have been playing lots of tennis."

"I'll put it on the left, you have good veins."

"Thanks. I'll take any kind of compliment. What color is it?"

"Hum, ah, oh, kind of a silver." In it went.

Henry is my dearest friend, but this mysterious little stainless steel box is my closest friend. A new lease on life: a pacemaker. My old ticker cannot go below 72 beats per minute, because when it tries, the pacemaker takes over. Miraculous. Same old atrial fibrillation, but not dangerous. Not even annoying.

* * *

Winter, 1993

Sometime in mid 1992, I realized I was awakening with acute shortness of breath, as if I'd been running a race. All sorts of tests ensued, which resulted in a new title: congenital heart failure. This title scared me into speechlessness. I presumed heart failure meant death. Newspaper notices often pronounce this "the cause of."

January 1993, I was back in the doctor's office. Breathing was more difficult at night and again I felt a great heaviness in my chest. More tests, and yet another title: pulmonary hypertension. I think that it means fluid leaking into the lungs. "Now," says he, "I want you to wear a Transderm nitro glycerin patch twenty hours per day and get some oxygen to use at night. These will help relieve the work of your heart. You'll live longer." I acquired the whole contraption, oxygen making machine et. al. I donned the line every night for three years. Took myself off of it with no ill effects.

* * * * *

Falling on Ice

The day before Christmas of 1989, I got last minute packages, including a newly framed painting, out of the car before Henry drove to town. Just before I reached the cottage my feet went out from under, on a patch of ice. I went down on my back and head—and could hear Hank drive away—unable to see me even if he had been looking because of deep surrounding snow. I was aware that I had broken no bones, that my hard head did not make me see stars. I tried to get up but was literally cradled by ice and couldn't get a footing or a hold on anything. Nobody was home. To my surprise I heard a loud howling and bawling. It was I, and I couldn't stop. I don't know how long I lay on the ice on my back with dripping ice coming down on me from the tree above.

Eventually I let go of the packages and crawled around and entered the cottage. My sobbing was so out of control I knew I should not be alone. I knew the Sheridan Burgesses were not at home. Jamie, ah, Jamie. I called Carol's house and managed to say I was okay but needed help. Jamie and Carol arrived thirteen minutes later and found me still standing by the phone with both hands, knuckles down, planted on the table. I kept telling myself to pick up my hands and sit down. Be sensible. But I could not move.

What a ghastly way to be found by anyone, let alone my son and his friend. But they were wonderful, got me to my own bed and washed the blood from a few cuts. I must have broken my fall with my elbows. I looked into Jamie's face to find him white as a sheet. Carol brought brandy and Band-Aids, and she gave me two Tylenol. When I finally subsided, Jamie's color returned. They stayed until Hank returned a half hour later. All this time my greatest dread was the embarrassment. I knew in the back of my mind that all my children and everyone else would know of my hysteria. Talk about injured self-esteem! Falling down is not for young old-ladies.

* * * * *

New York City

Ralston's wife, Mary Jane, died unexpectedly. It was early morning and my only thought was how expediently I could reach Babylon, which lies half way out on Long Island, New York. I was carrying a bunch of wild flowers, which I had gathered early that very morning. They became my last offering to my friend and sister-in-law.

Taking any plane I could, I landed at ten p.m. in Newark, New Jersey. Nearing midnight, still clutching my pitcher of wild flowers, I had already ridden on three airport shuttle buses, once to a parking lot, in quest of my non-appearing suitcase. The agent in the claims room very helpfully explained my route to the middle of Long Island via Port Authority bus into Manhattan, taxi to Penn Station, then the Long Island Railroad. No worry about my bag as it would turn up at the very door of my brother's house tomorrow. For a mad moment I considered asking if I could simply wait there and go with my bag.

Picking up my wild flowers I turned to leave the claims room. Someone gently plucked my sleeve. I looked up into the face of a man who simply said, "Wait outside. If my package is here I'll drive you into the City." I walked on out and turned to stare at his back. Tall and lanky, short gray hair, rimmed glasses. Plaid shirt with sleeves rolled up. Slacks and comfortable tan shoes. The quick glimpse of his face had bespoken a nice person. Yes, I would wait for him. It was not until much later that I realized that while I was judging him, he must have already judged me.

He came out with package in hand, again told me to wait, called to make sure of his delivery to 5th Avenue at 51st Street, then led me to his car. An old red two door affair, he cleared the back seat of tennis shoes. I never did understand why Flowers and I were ushered into Backseat. Frontseat was bare, only a rumpled blanket on the floor. When Tall and Lanky settled into the driver's seat he turned to me and made our positions quite clear. "I am a delivery man and this package contains computer parts, without which the business at 5th and 51st cannot open its doors tomorrow. You will wait in the car while I make the delivery, then I will take you to Penn Station and see you on the Long Island Train. Is that clear?" Yes, it was clear. We were off.

He regaled me with facts about buildings as we passed through Jersey City and Hoboken. The moon was not even out so I did not really see these sights, however the Statue of Liberty shown brilliantly, her back to us as she reached out towards the ocean. Then came the Holland Tunnel. Canal Street to Lafayette. Did

I know Lafayette was the beginning of Park Avenue? Little Italy. Chinatown. Union Square. This was Tall & Lanky's hometown and he was proudly showing her off.

At 5th and 51st the light was indeed burning in the window of the second floor. Did I want the car window up and doors locked while he was gone? No, not if he didn't think it was necessary. Several couples strolled by in the soft warm evening. Long gowns and tuxedos. Laughter. Alertness as they looked for passing cabs to hail. A scene from another decade, or so it seemed to me.

Proceeding back towards Penn Station I was told that if a guy felt real spiffy he might take his girl into Tiffany's. Did I know Best and Company was gone? Here is our public library, and certainly you have heard of B. Altman's. As he parked at Penn Station (I guess nobody calls it Pennsylvania) he explained the great new home of Madison Square Garden above the station. Descending to the labyrinth corridors we marched to the rack holding all train schedules where Tall & Lanky plucked out the one for Long Island Railroad. My next train gave me twenty minutes in the station. It was now 1:10 a.m. I was quickly led to the ticket counter where I duly purchased same and he pointed out Track 17. He announced I was hungry and led me to a snack stand where he graciously accepted a cup of coffee to go and ordered me a hot dog and orange soda to go. He was incredulous when I meekly mumbled that I would prefer milk and hot tea to orange soda. I really would also have preferred a sandwich but felt perhaps that was too great a change in his menu for me. He watched as I put the required mustard, catsup, and relish on the hot dog.

From there he took me to a phone booth right next to Track 17, told me to get out a dime and my brother's phone number and call so that I would not be waiting in the Babylon R.R. station at three o'clock in the morning. So I stood with dime, phone number, brown paper bag and Wyoming Wild Flowers as he formally shook my hand and gave me his name. I gave him my name and my husband's name and our home town in Wyoming. Please, John, come to see us one day. I watched John's receding figure stride out of sight.

* * * * *

A Cruise with Margery

Margery. My best friend since we were three years old. She is fair. I am dark. She likes to watch sports. I like to play sports. She is bandbox perfect. I like to let the wind blow through my hair. And so it goes, because our bond only grew stronger. We had terrible fights that devastated both of us. We were about ten or eleven when we finally outgrew them.

We have lived apart most of our lives, separated by various continents. But we each have a godchild of the other's. Our husbands became good friends. By letter and by telephone and visits, we shared our families' lives and our own ups and downs. We even took a theater trip to London, just the two of us, a couple of years ago. But none of this really prepared us for the startling revelations of our basic natures probably inherent since our births over seventy-five years ago.

Best friends for life, Mary and Margery, 1980

No, her husband did not wish to go on this cruise, but he encouraged her to join me. Of course we wanted a cabin with portholes, and a shower. Well, my friend thought she could go two weeks without a soak in a tub. Pretty soon she called back (we live on opposite sides of the U.S. of A.) to ask if we couldn't have a tub. Yes, we could have a tub with a shower. After all, she has a lousy back and I might like it, too. That put us up a deck and a monetary notch, or was it two? But her husband suggested we get more square footage in case we wanted to have a party. A what? And that put us on the swell promenade deck with a lovely bedroom and a sitting room, complete with refrigerator and shower/bath with a tub. It never occurred to us to have a party. I take that back. We dressed for one of the less "casual" nights and sought out a bar for company and a before-dinner drink. I still don't know why we couldn't find one, but we ended up back in our stateroom sharing the little C & O we had stashed, playing gin rummy, sometimes her version and sometimes mine. At eight thirty we descended to the Coral deck for dinner. We had chosen the second sitting so we wouldn't feel rushed.

Best of friends, we toured Venice: a gondola ride, a wander through the remarkable narrow streets and St. Mark's Square. As we were going through the Doges Palace I was vaguely aware that Margery stayed right up with the guide while I tended to linger, looking out the windows at the incredibly beautiful statues and domes in soft corals, off whites, grays and blue, turquoise greens against even a softer clear blue sky. We walked arm in arm along the canal to meet our tender and she remarked, happily, "This is like walking to grade school together."

The next day was at sea. I enjoyed the ship's pool while she had her hair done. Docking at Kusadasi we were invited to stroll the bazaars, find a bite to eat, then meet the bus at half past noon for a tour up to Ephesus. By eleven thirty we were sitting at an outdoor counter, the Turks' version of fast food, ordering lunch. Already my friend was muttering, "We must hurry," though the bus was a short distance.

We had an expert guide who made us feel the antiquity and graceful beauty of the ancient city of Ephesus. Then again we were left to browse for fifteen minutes, until bus time. I found myself intrigued as usual with the shops which are numerous around all bus stops. Margery gently said, "Mary, I'm, boarding the bus now." Say I, "Fine. I'll be along in a minute," as I noted nobody had boarded yet. But my eye was on the wrong bus, and ours was already moving out. I ran over and it paused long enough for me to hop on. And there was Margery standing in the aisle screaming, "You've got to keep up! You can't expect us all to wait for you!" This went on for five minutes, even after we were seated.

Yes, that was dumb of me. I also realized a great disparity in our innate personalities. She is always in front and I am always back yonder. Traveling with my family, they learned to accept that I would bring up the rear. Canoeing, hiking, biking, riding horseback, whatever—I was always last.

Margery would accept this. However, she had not counted on Capri. We were on top of a hill in a darling little city, again let loose, this time for two hours. It didn't take me long to find some byways, tiny twisting walled pathways. There were beautiful flowers and children with a parent. School was out. Just Margery and me, thoroughly lost. Poor Margery! "We'll be late. We'll never find them. They will have left us. How will we get back to the ship?" It didn't help to have me unconcerned. But following my nose I was sure we were all right. Yes, we were, but our party and our bus were nowhere to be seen.

Clever Margery held up a card that had the name of our restaurant. How could it be that so many locals didn't know it? A thoroughly exasperated Margery and a mute Mary finally found the gang, and they hadn't even missed us!

That evening I explained to my friend that we couldn't keep messing up each other. Just don't worry about me. I will be last, and you just go at your own pace also. "All right. We'll do that," said she.

Wintering

December 22, 1983

Henry has brought me tea and I asked him to open the curtains a bit, just to see what forty-five degrees below zero looks like. Well, it is beautiful and oh, so dangerous!

This is the coldest we've ever been, and it stays. Pipes have frozen but nothing burst. The heat and electricity were off for three hours one night, but all was okay. We are not quite snowed in, thanks to the tractor with a blade. Sheridan's feeding equipment won't start and only some of ours does. Jamie goes out on the snow machine (purchased just before this hit) which pulls a sled for salt block or hay, feed, etc., and he carries an ax to open watering holes and stock tanks which have frozen over despite immersed water heaters. The wind did that. Here at the Pony Track we have all the bulls, 950 calves, Sheridan's rams, two studs in different pastures, each with a friend (mares) and other assorted horses. Also a bunch of hospital calves—some got anti-something shots. One died of pneumonia. Jamie had to shoot the others suffering from coccidiosis. Before the advent of the grinder for hay and supplements to add to the hay, our calf crop would have been decimated. So far they are holding on.

Meantime, Sheridan feeds 1,100 cows, many sheep and probably thirty-odd horses and yearlings. Deer and antelope have mostly left for more protected areas. Big fat pheasants enjoy grain in the corrals. Chickadees hover outside our window for birdseed, but the opening to the feeder is frozen shut. White jackrabbits scurry and I even saw the comical ermine, which is a plain old weasel in summertime. Fox and coyote have burrowed in, around, and about. Other ranchers make out as we do, to a greater or lesser degree.

December 23

So here we are into tomorrow. Great progress yesterday. But there are still the discouraging moments when things inside feel worse rather than better. It is already eight a.m. So much outside is so critical that Henry is staying home to help and Jamie is vastly relieved. The temperature has risen fifteen degrees, to only thirty below! Even Fred, our son-in-law, came yesterday, dressed like an Eskimo with black silk scarf over nose and mouth, to take feed on the snowmobile to outlying horses. My only foray out of doors: I

Lookout Rock on The Divide

happened to be looking out in front and saw most of those calves trailing into the barnyard from across the creek and they were headed for the front meadow, which would never do. For once all my outdoor clothing was together so I slipped it on and ran past the bunkhouse, and with a mere hand clap and "poop-poop-dee-doop" they turned around and eventually re-crossed the bridge.

Jamie aches in every bone. I guess "bone weary" is the expression. However, he remains as cheerful as ever. He is still determined to bring back a Christmas tree.

December 24

Jamie finally brought in a Christmas tree. Three feet high with only two sides, the scrub cedar was just fine on a table with tiny lights. And hobbled Heather got a friend to pick her up for Christmas shopping, crutches and all, in ice and snow. Her present to me? She got her friend to shoot a porcupine! Presented it with a red ribbon around the middle. I took it to the taxidermist who wouldn't even look at it. I eventually tossed it. But I appreciated Heather's gesture.

December 25

Christmas dinner at our house. It took all day to keep machines working in the cold to feed the cattle. The kitchen sink was the only running water, but we all had a good time.

December 31

Henry's brother, Harry, died of cancer at age 73. The intense cold broke at last.

January 1

Henry and I flew to Abbeville, South Carolina for Harry's memorial, then we went to Margery and Bill's home on Sanibel Island for four wonderful days of rest and recuperation.

* * * * *

April 28, 1984

The granddaddy storm of them all. It caught everybody off guard—tractors in the fields for spring farming, husbands not home yet, travelers still on highways and byways. The relentless, paralyzing blizzard lasted three days and three nights. Ah yes, Henry was home, having brought an overnight guest out early. The guest, Davey Olmstead, became "the man who came to dinner" from Santa Fe. He left four days later on the rear of Henry's snowmobile with his elegant brief case and soft leather bag tucked in behind his city clothes, with tails flying. A friend from town, George Ewan, picked him up at the highway. Our lane was plowed out the following day.

No livestock could be fed or cared for. Snowmobiles were bogged down in the heavy but soft snow the first two days. I was exhausted just watching from the cozy living room fire. We did guest meals three times a day as we stayed quite formal with the man who was with Henry in the 11th Airborne. We lost a colt and a yearling horse, Sheridan's youngest lambs, and calves and many cows who got caught between drifts. We weren't hit as badly as the Basques south of us, whose sheep were wiped out.

Anyway, afterwards I dug under a two-foot drift and there were the daffodils still blooming. Spring is definitely on its way.

* * * * *

New Year's Day, 1990

The snow is very deep; dogs, cattle and man walk in hard won paths only. Henry wanted to drive out to where about forty heifers were stranded without any food and give them hay. He, Sheridan, and Lindy had gathered them by horseback two days before and taken them to an artesian well. I'm talking about beyond the NX, beyond the E—U, beyond the OTO ranches, to the corrals of the Scrutchfield Place maybe thirty miles from the Pony Track Ranch.

Though I could be of no help whatsoever I wanted to be company. Loaded with hay bales and Buffy, the border collie, on top of same, we left our ranch at nine thirty a.m. We were quite bundled and took water and crackers. Sheridan's four-wheel-drive pickup was our transport and the back window and the back side window were broken because the trailer had jack-knifed some weeks before. We passed no one going down the Prairie Dog Creek valley and certainly no one as we went up the Badger Creek valley, passing the NX. Then we did note and wave to David Kane who was feeding cattle at the E—U, and we drove through the Weigand Place, its dugout house long fallen in. We entered the OTO land and passed the deserted ranch and corrals, turning up the valley to take a narrow road to the artesian well. We were still in Wyoming but certainly on the edge of the world.

The heifers were fine and Henry unloaded some hay. It was still unbelievable to me that some rancher had a road patrol and had cleared this road enough for a single vehicle, but where to turn around? I decided I'd rather be out of the pickup, so indeed I watched Henry get stuck in the deep snow.

Now, I have learned through these many ranch years to take along a little entertainment for myself: a book, a magazine, knitting, or pen and paper for writing or drawing. This time I had a good book, and without saying a word, hopped back into the pickup and read while Henry shoveled around the wheels enough to put on chains. This kept me from telling him "how to do it" and to desist from "what ifs." Never fear when Henry's near, and we were on our way a half hour later.

We passed the OTO buildings when Henry decided to take the chains off. When he asked me to move the pickup just enough to get the chains off, we discovered it was dead and wouldn't start. Henry found a loose terminal under the hood but no wrench to tighten it. With no more ado he told me to stay in the cab and he would start walking. I said that if I got too cold I'd start walking too. I watched his back, black against the white snow, disappear down the road. Buffy couldn't stand it and trotted after him. He had a long walk ahead, to get beyond OTO property, through the Weigand Place, and finally reach the E—U house, which stands almost a mile off the road.

The day was overcast but not threatening. I put Sheridan's slicker over the broken window—kind of, anyway—an old pair of wool pants over my legs, wrapped my wool scarf around my head, hunkered down and resolutely read. Fortunately the story took place in a steamy jungle!

Sure enough, about an hour later here came Henry and David Kane in a nice warm pickup with a delighted Buffy in back. A twist of the terminal and jumper cables had us rolling once more. David was truly appalled when Henry walked up, but Henry was exhilarated by his four mile hike, infantry gait, fit as a fiddle. We were home by three o'clock, took hot showers, dressed, and picked up George Pearson to attend Pete Widener's open house. He had a beautiful spot at the foot of the Big Horns, about eighteen miles the other side of Sheridan. While others settled in to watch more football after the dismaying Rose Bowl, I found an easy chair with an ottoman and promptly went to sleep.

* * * * *

Christmas, 1990 and New Year's Day, 1991

Forty-eight degrees below zero. Head bolt heaters connected to the diesel Suburban and Henry's little gray pickup. Both are mired with gelled summer-weight fuel. We'd had such a lovely Indian Summer. Don, our foreman, patiently tried to start the diesel tractor to feed the cattle. But no luck. By dark he had completed what usually takes three hours.

Henry bundles in his warmest, having brought Maynard's bit into the house from the tack room to warm the metal before settling it into the horse's mouth. Then he rides through the calves and brings in a couple of them with pneumonia. Then Henry settles into the Cadillac which purrs like it's seventy degrees outside. I call it The Canoe, after Mops who called her Cadillac a canoe. He zooms over the hill to check the horses, to check the water tanks, out to check the bulls across the railroad track.

Sheridan calls. He has fifty degrees below, nor will his diesel tractor start. "Keep your eye on Dad," he says, "that car could get stuck." This brings to mind what Henry used to tell me to do about Sheridan himself. "When he rides horseback watch for him to return." But The Canoe has front wheel drive and Henry stays clear of snowdrifts.

This gives me a fine excuse to go to my studio, because it looks out onto the corrals and the bridge across Lower Prairie Dog Creek, to watch for comings and goings. I'm working on a large flower painting, acrylic on watercolor paper. And I'm becoming acquainted with sides three and four of *Cats*. I love it and wonder what happened to sides one and two. Mid morning Henry strides in bringing the cold of his clothes with him. "Do you see anything on my cheek? I think it is frost bitten." I do not see any color change but it seems to be numb.

Next day. Forty-eight degrees below zero and the Suburban and pickup still sit there like clunkers. Henry does not shave so that he keeps that last fine layer to protect his face, and follows the routine of yesterday. So do I. So does Don, whose last chore of the day is to put a tractor in the shed on the hill, not that it is warm, only that it is less cold. Then Don has to walk off the hill, across the bridge and over to the pickup. At such low temperature every activity becomes sluggish, kind of slow motion. And I, in the house, forever peering out, simply grow tired. I paint and wrap a last package or two.

Next day. Forty-five degrees below zero. Then up to twenty below. The pipes in the cottage, home of my studio, are frozen despite my having left the faucet trickling. It is Saturday but I call Donnie, and he and his helper come right out. The pipe to the cottage from the underground housing well is frozen. Of course he first had to shovel the snow off the opening, find a ladder and clamber down. That took the morning. Then he bent the float in the cottage toilet tank a little so it would keep the water on the move, not to worry about faucet drip anymore.

By two o'clock in the afternoon there is no water anywhere in the house itself, not even in the kitchen sink, which had never frozen. Also, the telephone is dead. Between those ongoing outdoor jobs, now routine to take all day, Henry goes up to Don's house and calls Donnie, who faithfully returns. A switch or something in the well house had switched off, simply turning off the water. By six o'clock in the evening we once again have water and a working phone.

About this time another look out the window shows Don pulling the diesel pickup towards the shop. Then he got behind with the little tractor and pushed it in, settling the tractor behind it. With that coddling the pickup started next morn and Henry got it out and let it idle much of the day to get rid of summer fuel. Then he skedaddled into town for "burner fuel" and it now runs on demand, with chains and hay bales to weight it. The Suburban was treated to the same warmth and fuel, so we drove it to the Planks' in Ucross for Christmas dinner. It carried us home in fine shape, but hasn't run since. The starter? The batteries?

Next day. The wind is up and it is not a Chinook. The pilot lights go off in the water tanks for the animals. Henry chops holes in the ice. He and Don slug through another day. Of course Sheridan does too, as do all other ranchers in the country.

Henry chopping holes in the ice

New Year's Eve. After a charming afternoon watching the Copper Bowl at Jack Ellbogan's, we find our phone dead again. I go back to town to Henry's office to phone somebody on the board of directors of the Range Telephone, but cannot unlock the funny lock at the office. It's not ten p.m. yet, but I head for the Ewans who are watching the six p.m. *Wheel of Fortune*, pushed back by the football game. I awoke Scotty Ferguson in Birney, Montana about the phone. Surely, he'd get somebody on New Year's morning.

New Year's Day. Mike Kuzara finally arrived at noon. He was relieved to find the cordless phone was at fault, not outdoor wiring. He unjacked it, and presto, all other phones on the go. Now, who was it I wanted to call?

After a warmish New Year's Day or so, we seem to settle for fifteen degrees below up to zero and even twenty above. Donnie was out again with a brand new holding tank for the well. The old one was full of "gunk," says he. But it couldn't be like the one that was here when we arrived thirty-two years ago and used for a few years. That had a dead rat or two. No wonder the children didn't like to wash their faces in it, let alone drink it.

So all was settled in, except that in the evening around nine thirty we realized that the heat was off in the house and cottage. No propane. Farmer's Coop came out immediately with fuel. We have two tanks and one was still full, simply turned off. However, the seven pilot lights had to be relit—one in Sheridan's darkroom in the old bunk house, another in the shop, four in the house, and one in the cottage. We were in bed by midnight.

It is now Sunday morn, January 6, 1991. The kitchen thermostat growls that it must warm the room, which is around fifty degrees, but it cannot connect. Oh, well, that too will get fixed sooner or later.

Checking the mailbox at the Pony Track Ranch

Henry

Washington, D.C., 1990

Saturday morning Henry and I decided to take the Metro from Foggy Bottom to the Smithsonian Institute to see the two new galleries. Already on the Metro, with more boarding at each station, were young couples with all their children, even babies. They were clean cut, well dressed in sport clothes, and in a holiday mood. At the Smithsonian we spewed out of the bowels of the underground. There were hundreds of these people with hundreds more already gathered above. Just before getting off the train we spied a sign. Anti-abortion. I became weak in the knees and trembled all over and soon dissolved into silent tears. In that split second of revelation I not only recognized these misguided people, but understood the hatred that engendered the War Between the States.

No cup of soothing tea was to be had, so we cut through the crowd now milling within the old museum to the beautiful garden atop the Sackler addition and found some sanctuary amongst the African and Oriental presentations. Henry grew restless and went outside while I finished viewing. Then I looked at every bench inside and out, retraced the maze of rooms. There was no sign of my man with his small Stetson. My only recourse—one hour later—was to simply take a cab back to our hotel. We drove along The Mall where thousands were now gathered. Picnickers and anti-abortion protesters everywhere. I recognize their right to demonstrate, just don't let them get close to me.

Henry and I arrived at our room about the same moment. We eyed each other a little warily and quickly opted for lunch. Well, it was one thirty. I guess it was a combination of our forty-four years together and not wanting to spoil our precious and precarious time that we avoided a confrontation. Iced tea for him and a Manhattan for me as he explained his waiting for me at one museum (not long I think) then taking a hike. He was exhilarated by his one hour walk from the Smithsonian to Foggy Bottom.

After delicious broiled scallops we took our wordless, reserved, tender reunion time together. Napped, showered, and dressed, we sauntered the three blocks to the Kennedy Center, and munched on a delightful sandwich. It was fun to be amongst theater goers and look at the latest fashions, knowing that many of these people actually lived in the Capital. There was not an empty seat in the Eisenhower Theatre, where we were thoroughly entertained by "The Cemetery Club," a play that moved to Broadway that May. It was a healing evening.

* * *

Oh, my, what a lusty man I have—thank God.

To love, to make love, to be loved. To define it in sexual embrace. The power it has for us to heal, renew, release, encourage—refilling triumphant.

The core of our existence together. From which stems every nuance of our internal and external relationship. The more Henry is involved with other people, places, and problems, and the more I become involved with children and my own activities, the race to live each hectic day requires understanding and endurance at every turn for both of us. Sometimes I think we are not traveling on the same road at all. Sometimes we are so irritated with each other we cannot speak, let alone make love. Lying in the same bed one of us will tentatively touch the other. Perhaps there is a response; perhaps the other is not yet ready. So we wait for each other, hating it, shielding our hurts, continuing to accede to our demanding daily jobs in pain and with impatience. The testing of wills, divergent philosophies of child raising, sometimes of how to handle holidays and the sacred rites of Christianity, the deep traditions of our growing up. Good heavens. Henry and I are more or less from the same economic background, ethnic and ethical, too. Education, travel, even war. If we find it sometimes tenuous, what must it be like for those of dissimilar persuasions?

The will to succeed, to let go of pride, to unfetter one's mind from past hurts and offenses, to accept the other's faults and less attractive habits and by the same token, attempt to diminish one's own failings—the daily challenges and commitment we make to each other. Then the touch that finds response; the utter joy of acceptance once again.

Henry: "I never want to just take. I want you to be with me all the way. Always."

I do not know how it is for Henry or another man, or for other women. But for me to give and to take sexually I must have a small space of time, regardless of which hour it is out of the twenty-four. I need this in the presence of Henry, quiet and undemanding yet expectant on his part. I take this time to momentarily rest my body for the pleasure and need it is about to give and receive. More important is what is happening in my mind.

In our first few years of marriage we had no minds, only bodies. Now the first thing to do is clear my mind of our children, our home, all things pertaining to our daily life. Then I cast out all taboos and inhibitions—these must have been what Mother hinted at. I gradually enter into the secretive, ever mysterious, repellent, most enticing and compelling world of sex. Then I turn to my husband who has through the years learned to use and care for me and my moods with great sensitivity. To take my body with such relish and fastidious exploration and approval in all he finds in me gives to me the glorious—yes, triumphant—ability to seek the same in him and his body, to exhibit before him my own desires—indeed to take as well as to give. We no longer scoff at Linda's remark made on our honeymoon. Ten years indeed.

It was so easy then. No thoughts except Mother's permission (perhaps). Then the acquisitions began. Material needs—and wants. Baby needs—and demands. Social—ah, social.

The art of setting forth as a couple. Of observing one another's being in the presence of others. What a shock. Other conversations, years ago:

Henry: "I wish you wouldn't look so bored when I'm telling a story just because you've heard it before."

Mary: "Do I look all right?"

Henry: "You look elegant. And I love to look at your legs and ankles in high heels."

Mary: "Did I talk too much? Too loud?"

Henry: "Well, yes, dear—a little. And must you flirt so outrageously? Do you forget you are married to me?"

Mary: "Gosh, never do I forget that. I guess I just trained myself in the Red Cross."

Henry: "Will you ever be ready to go on time?"

Mary: "Well, I can never decide about jewelry until the last minute. My hair wasn't quite dry. Had to kiss all the children. Sitter instructions. Lights and heat up or down. But I'll try."

Henry: "I danced with all the ladies and had a great time. But always best to dance with you."

Mary: "And I'm so glad you danced with the ladies, because then their husbands dance with me. And so good to be dancing with you once again."

Both of us: "Aren't we lucky that we both love to dance, and that Sheridan has so many dancing parties?"

Gypsies at a Beaux-Arts ball

St. Patrick's Day. Green hair for both of us.

My homemade vest from the cute beaver who nibbled down three young trees right outside the bathroom window.

* * *

Henry, My Falling Star

December, 1994

Banana peels go into the freezer, sometimes the refrigerator, or into his pockets as he prepares to take his early morning walk with Charlie, his young black Labrador retriever. But tonight it is eleven thirty as they leave the house. For the moment I have hidden the bananas in the breadbox, so he has two apples.

This morning I did some errands on my own. Any phone calls? None, says he. However, Sheridan called this evening and said he talked to Dad this morning. No matter. Sheridan will take him to the ranch to look over the cattle while Sheridan feeds tomorrow.

This afternoon Henry, Charlie, and I went to see Eleanor, our bookkeeper. We are so grateful for her cheery welcome and her sorting of our bills so simply. As the bills arrive I hide them so there will be no confusion. Henry gets to sign the checks. That makes him feel important.

I try to have us go somewhere every day. After Henry's early one hour walk, he is not eager to go out to walk again. He changes his clothes, then usually takes a nap, and it is only nine thirty or ten a.m.

Early morn, sometimes there is already a ray of light from the East. I have come to realize that Henry spends at least one hour just meandering about the house before he dresses. Another hour, sometimes, before he is actually out the door, bundled to the teeth. I have learned not to disturb him, not to help him. Just to lay low, even as he paces our bedroom, gazes out each window, walks down the hall, comes back. When he is finally ready he always returns to kiss me and waves in farewell. Charlie seems to do the same.

Henry changes his clothes several times a day. He may come out in his underwear topped by his cavalry hat, or perhaps just his undershirt and big cowboy hat. He is not trying to be funny. I suggest at least underpants. "Well, I don't know where they are." I open his top drawer. Lots of them, all neatly bundled with rubber bands. As are his socks. As are his sweaters. Coats are tied with rope or belts. And these all float from drawer to closet shelf to drawer. No wonder he can't find underpants.

I know not to ask him where anything is. If a book or paper seems to be missing it may turn up in an hour, or a day or two, or never. So I watch the mail carefully. I no longer ask if he would like to put something in the mailbox if I have put something in earlier. He will always put down the red flag and bring the outgoing mail into the house.

It is now December 13, twelve fifteen a.m. He and Charlie have returned. By golly, he is drawing his bath. Trouble is, he slept hard for a couple of hours earlier. Well, so did I, which is why I'm awake also.

The next morning. So he is taking another walk. Again bathed and well shaven. He takes care to brush his teeth daily. About his clothes: was it ten or twelve years ago when I first noticed that the underwear and sock drawer was no longer tidy? It simply became a swirl. It was not until he started on medication last spring that he began to organize his clothes by bundles with elastic bands.

Was it then or earlier that there were subtle and unsettling changes in behavior at the office? I will ask Janet, his long time loyal and affectionate secretary.

We have a big plastic container into which we put cat food. I had printed "CAT" on all four sides. Henry came out with it filled with dog food. I said, "But this is dog food." He testily replied, "No, it isn't. It says "CAT" right here!" I could only laugh at his interesting logic. He laughed too, but he didn't know why.

It was with dread that I faced packing to take the six a.m. flight on the day after Christmas, to visit our daughter Molly and her family in Texas. Dread not only for me, but for him who had always been his own good packer. In fact, I didn't begin until ten p.m. the night before. Even then, only my bag. Got up at four thirty a.m. to pack for Henry. He carried his bag to the car, then mine. Very cooperative, he grabbed his hat and my coat. Of course, I held the tickets, had made the decision of when we'd go, when we'd return, even that we'd go at all. Henry had always made those decisions. I planned this trip "with" Henry, who always listened intently. He had even planned, and he watched Sheridan take Charlie to the car to stay at the ranch. Yet in the predawn on the way to the airport he asks, "Where are we going?" And when we arrive in Texas and start to unpack he begins to put things back in his bag. "Well," says he, "aren't we going home?"

Now we have been with Molly's family for three days. He is content. He is entertained by the boys and by watching Molly work out at the fitness club. Then he asks, "Where is the male of this family?" Hayden shares his walks. He listens quietly while Matthew plays his guitar. We are both happy to hear the sounds of a busy home. I play cards with the family in the evenings. Henry wanders around us quietly, simply enjoying.

* * *

Mary Hayden Burgess

February, 1995

Henry points to his feet and says, “Ride, riding.” He is wearing his walking shoes. “Boots,” say I. We both grin. Not his riding boots, but boots anyway—they are at the cobblers getting new heels.

I have tried to get him to put banana peels in the sink for the Dispose-All instead of the wastebasket. He doesn’t get it. I prowl the wastebasket for the odiferous peels, realizing this is something he cannot learn. However, lately, I know he comprehends that I don’t want them in the wastebasket, because they turn up on the lawn.

It used to be that when he didn’t like my driving, I’d simply stop and say, “You drive.” Now that I am the sole driver I appreciate the fact that he only says, “You are a good driver.” Yes, I do drive more carefully, more thoughtfully, so he doesn’t lose confidence in my ability.

He likes to push the cart in the grocery store, following behind me. Ah, how many other couples do I observe in the same pattern. If he disappears I know he has gone for bananas and, uncannily, he knows where they are. And at the other end of the store he can get the oatmeal raisin cookies he loves.

Henry is in and out of lucid awareness. Where is the east door? The patio? Which end has the curtain cords? However, he ritualistically closes all at night. He keeps all doors closed. He always asks if he can help me. Then he cannot, or forgets. He makes his bed. He sleeps half of most nights with me, then goes down the hall to another bedroom. He turns lights on and off during the night, but leaves me undisturbed. Not only does he look in upon me, as I sleep later than he, but Charlie does, too. When I’m in the bathroom Charlie will just glance in to make sure I’m there, as does Henry, the way our little children used to.

Just lately he has snapped at me. Well, I snapped back. This puts us both in tears and full of apologies. I will try to do better. It is time for me to make this five day trip to La Jolla, California to visit Elizabeth and Larry, who have been together now for fifty-eight years.

Henry is still meticulous in personal cleanliness, shaving, bathing, etc., but forgets to comb his hair. A small matter, but it used to be well brushed, always.

Henry follows me into a store. I purchase whatever while he waits by the door. I greet him on the way out and say, "Okay, let's go." He is ready. But when I get to the car, he is not behind me. He is still just standing inside. I find that when we are going somewhere in the car I must not forge ahead to the car. I will find myself waiting for him. I go back into the house to discover he is just standing there, waiting also. The irony of it all is that for most of our forty-nine years he has sat in the car waiting for me. On the other hand, if I am not quite ready but tell him where we are going, he will get into the car and start the motor for me, with the garage door still shut.

* * *

Fisher's Island – August, 1995

Dear Kate,

I am sitting in a comfortable chair on the lawn in front of Sally's lovely gray-shingled house tucked into the land on a bluff above the Sound. Sally is my friend from Red Cross days. I see Montauk, the end of Long Island, to my right and scan the horizon to spot Block Island rather leftish. The lazy waves are slapping large rocks below. The rocks give way to a fine sandy beach in a protected cove. We swim here each day. The sun is kind with the slightest of breezes.

When first I entered the water I felt the freedom of being unfettered by the walls of a pool. As I so often do, I dipped my head under to swim beneath the surface. Unbidden came a realization that I was free from Death—for the first time since 9:00 a.m. April 4th of this year.

How beholden I had become to that day and the day before and the months since. I am yet unable to envision Amos before that time. People say I have wonderful memories of life with him. I am sure I do, but they are still locked away. In the devastation of the loss of my mate, I realize I am locked into grief.

The desk where I thought I would start to write this has a mirror facing the writer. I looked into it inadvertently and saw Sadness staring back. I burst into tears and sobs such as I have for the most part been unable to do at all.

It was a release and a relief to do so. But I put pen and paper away. I joined Sally and another guest, Alice Meade, for a light drink before dinner. I was relaxed and wore a smile in the pleasure of their company.

Sally's summer house turns out to be one big house party with all sorts of friends and relatives coming and going. After all, it has five bathrooms plus two half baths, and eight bedrooms, if I've counted correctly. The kitchen hub is presided over by Claire Sullivan, recently graduated from Boston College and soon to be a CPA in Boston. Sandwiched in between is the airy large rectangular living room, from the high ceiling of which hangs a real Calder mobile.

I am aware that any and all "know" about Henry, but no one says a word. They are just gentle, and because they never knew him, I feel a sense of being anonymous. At home a certain notoriety surrounds me. I am the widow of the man who shot himself. People look at me out of the corner of their eye. I know how they speculate. Not unkindly, you understand, but wondering what the whole scene was like, how I am coping, what I am thinking. I don't blame them, as I would do the same. I do feel surrounded by protective sympathy. I get a hug from a near-stranger, a kiss or a handshake from friends and acquaintances who've not seen me since April 4th, 1995 at 9:00 a.m. I'm asked, "How are you?" To which I usually reply, "Very Well, Thank You."

The phone rings, from Anywhere, USA. "Just want to know how you are doing." Periodic calls from locals, also. If I were very truthful I would reply, "I have no idea of how I am. Ask me a couple of years from now."

I still catch my breath when I look in the mirror each day and behold the face that Henry looked at with such love, such intensity, such longing and sorrow the evening of April 3rd. He caressed my face and kissed me so softly. He was insistent and utterly silent. All so different than any other time in our forty-nine and a half married years. I did not know until the next morning that he was saying goodbye, goodbye.

Maybe he thought he'd do it that night or at dawn. He was up early, as usual, and took Charlie for their walk. As usual, I had my cup of tea in bed, wrote a letter and was making phone calls. Henry returned and lay down on his back next to me and kicked off his shoes. He seemed to snooze, but now I don't know. But then, I often didn't know.

Henry sat up. He said, "I am no longer any good to my country or my town. I am no good to my children and I am no good to you."

By now we were standing and he took my face into his hands the way he had the night before. Then he stomped down the hall as he said, "I have this problem and it won't go away. I'm going to shoot myself." I stood still, wondering if he would remember what he just said, what he had said three times in the last four years. I started down the hall, heard the gun, then heard his body fall.

He was lying on his back, partially in the kitchen. The tiniest hole in the middle of his forehead. No blood on his face. His old .22 rifle flung away from his hand. Charlie staring at him. I lay down beside him and told him "I love you" even as I knew he had already gone yonder.

* * *

September 4, 1995

It has been five months to the day. I scrutinized my face in the mirror. I see it is no longer exactly the one that Amos looked at so longingly and with the intensity I could not fathom at the time. It is older, for one thing. Fisher's Island tanned it. Well, intensified my freckles. The lines seem to be deeper and my eyes look back at me reminding me of the complete reality of life. I used to be such a daydreamer, but that wonderful protective shell has disappeared, actually long before Amos' death.

During our three and a half years of correspondence during the war I always wrote, "Dear Amos." I spoke to others of him as Amos, his middle name. And he would sign his letters Amos. Not until we met again did he tell me how he always disliked that name. But now, if I wish, I can call him that, in this writing anyway. It has a secret coziness to it.

* * *

June 22, 1997

Dear Henry,

I've been thinking about our night walks up the lane. So still, so black, so softly warm with shimmering stars falling all the way to earth. On moonlit eves we could watch the meadow alfalfa once more waiting for the dawn to eventually burst into a profusion of purple blossoms, and for the bees to take their due. We often went up the lane in the pickup with trailer hauling a heifer to the vet to have her calf delivered safely by Caesarian. Those nights could be shimmering with stars, maybe softly warm, but in the spring it could also be icy cold, or storming snow or rain. One spring our cows had thirteen Caesarians. We finally realized those Angus bulls had been bred larger, so they were throwing larger calves. And the only reason we put Angus with our basically Hereford herd was to make for easier calving.

How often I walked the lane to meet the children or see them off to school. With different dogs and different little ones by my side. And I still walked the lane when Jamie was the only one left at home.

The backbone of our life together: thinking of them every single day. I asked you, "Would we have moved out to the ranch if we had no children?" "Why no, we would not."

They are baptized and confirmed into the Episcopal church. They all have college degrees. Beyond that they are on their own. Singly and collectively they are beautiful.

* * *

For weeks after Henry died I took several baths a day. My footsteps were leaden. I did not read a paper or magazine. Still too stunned to cry. But then one time when all alone in the house, I started howling until I could howl no more. A modicum of relief.

After Daddy's death, I found solace in howling in an open field. When Sarah died, I went deliberately to a pasture in the hills behind the ranch house.

I did not howl when Mother died. She was ninety and her time had come—actually, had come a few years earlier. When I got the news, Henry and I were in California attending a reunion of people interned by the Japanese in the Phillipines during World War II. We were standing at a bar with loud jazz playing, about to sip our drinks. An ex-internee, a missionary, came up to us. She already knew and said, "Let us bow our heads in prayer." We set down our drinks and prayed. The band played on.

Not until she was gone did I realize that all the tugging that went on between us through the years was Mother's effort to protect me. She was my Protector.

* * *

Two years after Henry's death I ran away from home, to Denver where Heather and her son Raby lived.

She found Park Place, a retirement community, for me. Henry remained anonymous, and I did too. I was always aware that the Rockies lay to the west and gave me a tenuous hold on Sheridan. I kept my Wyoming driver's license and license plates.

I tried to paint but could not. Made some good friends, and found Denver an intriguing city.

After three and a half years Heather and Raby moved to Minnesota. I was restless anyway, and came back to Sheridan and to our son Sheridan and his family, who keep me anchored.

I am content.

* * *

Mary and Henry, 1994

* * *

Henry Amos Burgess, 1918 - 1995

Henry A. Burgess was born on August 22, 1918, in Sheridan, Wyoming, to Judge James H. Burgess and Helen Helvey Burgess, joining his eight-year-old brother, Charles. The Burgess family lived in Sheridan, but spent most of their time on the family ranch, the <u>NX</u>, twenty-five miles northeast of Sheridan.

Henry attended Linden Elementary School and graduated from Sheridan High School in 1936, where he served as class president for four years. He followed in his brother's footsteps by going to Harvard in the fall of that year. He spent one summer in Cuba, and the following summer he attended classes at the University of Munich, Germany. Convinced there might be a war in the offing, he returned home, and during his last year at Harvard he joined the 115th Cavalry of the Wyoming National Guard. With correspondence classes and summer training programs, he entered the Guard as 2nd Lieutenant while still a student.

Henry graduated from Harvard in 1940, and that fall he entered his father's Alma Mater, the University of Michigan Law School in Ann Arbor. During his first semester, however, the Wyoming National Guard was called to active duty at Fort Lewis, Washington, and his law degree was put on hold until after World War II. The horse Cavalry was then mechanized and disbanded, and in 1941, Henry joined the 11th Airborne Parachute Infantry Division of the US Army. Henry's distinguished military career in New Guinea, The Philippines and Japan included the rescue of over 2,000 American civilians held captive over three years in the Los Baños Prison Camp south of Manila. Lieutenant Colonel Burgess was awarded the Bronze Star, the Purple Heart, the Silver Star and Legion of Merit before being honorably discharged in 1945.

Henry had met Mary Hayden of Ann Arbor, Michigan, the summer of 1941, while still a lieutenant in the 115th Cavalry, and on January 19, 1946, Henry and Mary were married. Henry then returned to Michigan Law School and they began their family, first with son Sheridan and thirteen months later, daughter Molly. Henry graduated from Michigan Law in 1949. He brought his young family back to Sheridan, Wyoming, where he began a successful law practice that continued for the next forty years. He and Mary subsequently added three more daughters, Tyler, Heather and Sarah, and another son, Jamie.

In returning to Wyoming, Henry also returned to ranching, and in addition to his law practice, Henry operated a working cattle ranch for thirty-five years. The family moved to the Pony Track

Ranch seven miles outside of Sheridan in 1956, where the children were raised and where Henry and Mary remained until illness forced them to move back into Sheridan in 1991.

Henry also served in the Wyoming House of Representatives and the State Senate, and he served a term as Sheridan County Attorney. Another of Henry's community activities was long time service on the Board of Whitney Benefits, Inc. As a member of the Trial Lawyers of America, Henry had studied Inverse Condemnation. Whitney Benefits owned the mineral rights of a large tract of land and had contracted with Peter Kiewit Company to mine the coal. The application for a permit to mine was rejected because the coal lay in an alluvial valley. Henry urged Whitney and Kiewit to sue the U.S. Department of Interior for compensation for the value of the coal which could not be mined. Representing Whitney Benefits, Henry started this litigation in 1973 and pursued it through the District Court, the Wyoming Supreme Court, the Federal Court, the U.S. Court of Claims, the U.S. Court of Appeals, and back to the Court of Claims. In 1995 the Court ruled in favor of Whitney Benefits and Peter Kiewit. Whitney's share of the settlement plus compound interest amounted to $64,000,000. Henry was active in the 11th Airborne Association and was its president for four years.

Henry Burgess died one week before this announcement was made. On April 4, 1995, Henry took his own life. He had suffered from Alzheimer's disease.

Final Words

Musings

In time, life changes one's outlook and behavior. For me, a mellowing, more tolerant view of the world. I'm more positive about many things. And yet, I feel more questioning about others about which I used to feel so certain.

Do I believe in God? Nine days after Sarah died the all-enveloping aura of God gently left me. I did not know He was even with me through all those harrowing days and nights until the moment of His departure. I was given to understand that I could now hold my own. This was so private, so internalized, so direct an episode with God that I mentioned it to no one. However, I finally knew I had to share this with my best friend, so I confided in Henry. He looked at me incredulously and exclaimed he had received the same message the same day and that he was fully aware of God's presence.

Do I believe in Jesus? A Christian is one who believes that Christ died upon the cross in propitiation for our sins. That He is the intermediary for God. As a Sunday School child I did learn that our church, St. Andrews Episcopal Church in Ann Arbor, is in the shape of a cross. As a church squirmer, with Mother bringing pencil and paper for me to doodle on during the sermons to keep me quiet, I was often concerned about what my sins might be. I couldn't understand the meaning of many of Moses' Commandments. "Covet," "adultery," "idols" and so on were words beyond my comprehension and made me feel ignorant. But it relieved me to know I had not killed anyone, even though I knew Daddy had once killed a snake. "Conception" and "Holy Ghost" were from a never-never land. I finally was able to remember "ascended" means going up and "descended" means going down, sort of like an elevator. I was impressed that Jesus' mother had my name and His father had Daddy's name. I felt important, because it was Mary and Joe, not Betty and Joe, Betty being Mother's name. She had been left out. Why?

One day before Easter, when in the sixth grade, we saw the movie *King of Kings.* For me, there will never ever be anything more violent, more heart breaking, more shocking. The triumph of Easter morning has never reached me after the violence of the Friday before, as depicted in this movie. Even as a so-called grownup I have been unable to accept Easter as anything but the saddest day of the year, though it encompasses some of the world's greatest music, which I love, and is the Christian's most triumphant day.

Now that I am "big" and understand the meaning of each of the Ten Commandments, and probably have a few real sins upon my head, I still realize that following these rules does not a Christian make. They are a code for conduct and most, or all, are incorporated in other religions also. Jesus is a wonderful leader, a great comforter and advocate of God. The concept has imbued the multitudes through the centuries with faith and courage.

However, God came to us very personally when Sarah died and was unaccompanied. Positively. Privately. Absolutely.

As a teenager I could be found weeping in church for the beauty of ritual. During the war I often sought out a church or cathedral to give me peace. On Easter morning, 1943, in Cambridge, England, I found the College's stone church, but the door had closed. The hymns had begun. I listened intently behind the closed door, but did not hear a female voice, so dared not enter. Easter of 1944 found me in Penzance watching a dress parade by a regiment of the 29th Infantry Division.

The Episcopal Church has been an integral part of my life since I can remember. At St. Andrews in Ann Arbor I was christened, Sunday Schooled, and attended church regularly, all with parents, grandparents, a few friends and relatives. I loved the simple pomp, the strong large choir made up of men and women and boys, including Ralston and my father. The organ was awesome, as was the long, tiled aisle leading to the gas-lit candelabras before the entrance to the altar. Weddings, funerals, christenings, Christmas Eves.

Ah, Christmas Eves. Those wonderful memories.

* * *

I have no concept of what lies beyond death. I do know that all of life is an adventure, made up of good deeds and misdeeds, mistakes and corrections, good health and ill—all manner of highs and lows and safe middles. Relationships with all kinds of people throughout life are among its greatest adventures.

I am no intellectual, but I do appreciate the written word, artistic endeavors of all sorts, and consider such to augment a richer comprehension of the philosophy of life. Education is never wasted no matter how one might stray from an original purpose, because it remains intrinsic. Competitive sports mostly enhance one's sensibilities to fair play, learning to win and lose with grace and a further self-knowledge. One usually strives to do the very best, even when not exhibiting or competing. Favorite recreations give balance to what might be humdrum. And there is nothing wrong with just walking.

Parasailing with George Ewan over Bora Bora

* * *

Summation

I have wallowed in the "Seas of Despond." I know the terrifying and destructive nature of jealousy. I have known the passion of hatred, which has nothing to do with "I hate this furniture" or "I hate this food." I have been filled with self-doubt, remorse and regrets, and have felt extreme shyness.

I have experienced the ecstasy of physical love, and the tenderness of true love and friendship. I have yelled like a fishmonger's wife, and sung lullabies to my babies, and rubbed the backs of children and grandchildren of all shapes and ages. I know anger in all its intensity, and the pure joy of being alive with the untold riches of a good and eventful life, a remarkable husband and exceptional children. I have longed for rest and oblivion, and have been thrilled by the stunning sunsets of the world.

When Henry and I eventually moved from the ranch back into Sheridan, I had a lovely studio, a room all to myself at 1808 Fairway Lane. While at the ranch, I discovered I could not paint when Henry was home. I would think that he was off in the hinterlands by pickup or horseback and suddenly there he'd be, and painting was done for the day. It was frustrating, so I simply made myself a rule that I do not paint when Henry is home. I also tried to finish up for the day before the children came home from school. Back in town, when it was impossible to paint there, I rented a little studio downtown above NZ's shoe store. I loved that little place. I inherited a bright orange velveteen sofa. I could look out those long narrow windows in the back towards the Big Horn Mountains.

After Henry's death, I thought I was going to go right on painting in my little studio downtown. But my painting there was completely different than anything else I'd done. I don't know whether it's any good or not, but I have never really gotten back into it. I have tried several times. Over the thirty-five or more years I was painting, I managed to sell maybe hundreds of paintings, enough to keep me in supplies and friends.

I would like to think that painting will again be a central part of my life, although one day, painting with Alice, I don't know how long ago, maybe a year and a half after Henry's death, she said, "Mary, you just can't paint anymore." Maybe she's right, but I want to give myself the opportunity of challenging that remark. Maybe it will be a different style. Can't go back.

Grief has no boundary, but I don't cry anymore. And I have learned to laugh again.

* * *

P.S. My Journey Up the Amazon River

Wednesday, September 26, 2001

This day George Ewan and I flew to Miami. The next day we checked in at the airline with our tickets, IDs and passports, which included and a visa to enter Brazil and proof that we had had a yellow fever shot.

And *then…*

Much to our consternation, it was discovered I had inadvertently picked up my old, outdated passport! Seeing our speechless and horrified expressions, the kindly agent pulled strings to let me fly to Port-of-Spain, Trinidad, off the coast of Venezuela. Innocents that we are, we thought I was home free when we boarded the *Clipper Adventurer*, having bussed right from the airport in Trinidad.

The purser picked up our passports. She noted mine and suggested I get someone to pick up my current one and send it posthaste to Cayenne, the capital of French Guinea, to arrive no later than noon, October 3. From the ship, I called Barbara Walter back in Sheridan. She spent all the next day getting it off...UPS Express.

And *then…*

I discovered my suitcase was still in Miami. We had a day in Trinidad so I had a half-hour to find a change of clothes. I picked up a rayon pantsuit, a long flowered skirt, a black top, and a bathing suit, all locally made. I was wearing sport shoes and George was carrying my bathing slippers, black and unstylish. My large purse carried meds, nightie, lipstick and powder, toothbrush, brush, traveler's checks and, of course, a good book. All set.

The next couple of days we explored the Orinoco River. High tide and muddy with silt. Our ship anchored in the river. We boarded zodiacs, those rubber rafts, to travel up estuaries to discover birds and a sloth. The jungle came to the water's edge except where it was chopped out to allow the river people to put up shanties: a floor on stilts, a roof, and several hammocks. The women and children stared at us as we stared at them. The river people make long narrow canoes out of tree trunks, scooping out the inside. So graceful. Wearing life preservers and coolest of clothes, we exuded not perspiration but real sweat in the humid heat.

Mary and George

Mary Hayden Burgess

Wednesday, October 3

We anchored in the bay at Iles du Salut, France. These are three tiny islands in the Atlantic Ocean, off the coast of French Guinea. By zodiac we landed at the small dock at Isle Royale. We walked around the whole seventy acres, sweating but intrigued. George and I followed our guide's example and ate a couple of termites. Crunchy. Had a cool drink at the old Auberge Hotel at the top of the hill. Near by is the infamous Devil's Island. The other island, St. Joseph, is just as infamous, both harsh penal colonies at the turn of the century. French criminals and politicos were sent here, mostly to die. Did you ever read the book, or see the movie *Papillion*? Do you know the story of Alfred Dreyfus?

No amount of cajoling by the *Clipper* folk was going to induce Brazil to let me in without a current passport. And who knows where that important little document is at this writing? The ship is headed for the Amazon this very afternoon at four p.m. The purser gave me a backpack for my sundries, but it took no time at all to pack. Three thirty p.m.

And *then*...

I was Deported! Time to leave this delightful ship with a great crew. Time to leave George at the little deck to a waiting zodiac to whisk me to the dock at Ile Royale. There I met Christian, *Clipper*'s Cayenne agent. We boarded a small boat called a ferry with three other dark French-speaking fellows. As we passed the *Clipper Adventurer* I stood out on the foot-wide deck, hung on to a bar, and waved heartily to people on the deck. As we passed the bridge, the captain and his mates waved back then gave me three blasts on the ship's horn. I was thrilled.

Deported!

On the mainland, an hour and some away, Christian ushered me into his little Renault—without air-conditioning—and we headed for Cayenne. Jungle, but often open land. The two-lane highway was well maintained.

Christian had booked me into a modern hotel. My bedroom at the top of the first floor was air-conditioned. I swept down the stairs in my lace-trimmed wild skirt, black linen shirt and ugly black slippers. The lobby, the bar, the lounge, and the dining room are not air-conditioned. Many fans whirl overhead from the high ceilings. Gentle breezes waft through the wide-open rooms. Palm trees sway outside. Somerset Maugham, where are you?

I took to writing this journal during the cocktail hour so I would not look so alone as I sipped a bit of rum. Notice I did not say "lonely." Moved to the spacious dining room. I was unable to judge the French menu or French-speaking dark waiters. I ordered far too much. No matter. In the morning Christian will sort out a plane to Miami. I hope to meet my suitcase there. I have thought about my carefully planned bag and realize we don't need much. But I would have liked having my camera and good walking shoes. I hope George is enjoying the Amazon. I never contemplated his joining me in my abandonment, nor did he offer.

Thursday, November 4

Slept well. Breakfast is bountiful. Other diners are mostly white and French, very casually dressed. The men all seem tall, have flat tummies, and many sport dashing mustaches *á la* Fred Mooney. The ladies stand tall, too, with enviable carriages. Their clothes are skintight. I know what they have. Youth.

Ah, a man calls and says I can fly to Miami on Saturday. It leaves at noon but I must be there three hours ahead. I wonder: how far to the airport? I slept the day away. Late afternoon I went into the lovely pool wearing my new one-piece suit. I looked over the sunbathers and swimmers. I was overdressed. Couldn't go earlier because sunscreen is in my suitcase and they sell none here. At the bar I copy a drink someone else is having: one inch grenadine, one inch sweet soda, topped with Heineken beer on tap. Delicious.

I am glad I have my own book. Magazines, papers and books are in French, of course. My high school French has evaporated with the years. In fact I did not have a conversation with anybody for four days. Have you ever thought about four days in your life being completely anonymous, with nothing expected of you, no decisions to make, doing only what you want to do? And in such a lovely setting? I did not even call my children. Let them think I am sweltering on the Amazon.

Friday, November 5

It is Friday and at last Christian calls to say he has my proper passport. Guess what. My passport arrived in Guyana Tuesday evening, but Christian did not pick it until Thursday! What goes? But you were right on, Barbara, and so was UPS. Christian sounded triumphant because I couldn't leave his country without it. Indeed,

I showed it four times. Cayenne has a fine airport, all metal. There is the European Space Center at nearby Kourou. Air France lifted off on schedule. We dropped down at Martinique, then Guadeloupe. Will be in Miami soon. We were on the ground at Guadeloupe…

And *then*…

"Everybody off! Here is your pass to get on again. A crew change." We waited in another handsome airport. And we waited. There was a large crowd of Haitians, mostly medical students returning from a month in France. After three hours a large Haitian began to harangue the people. No authority was to be seen. Police came, then those men in black with shin and knee guards, helmets, truncheons and guns. Are we in a play? Another hour goes by. A very efficient French woman herds us out to three big buses, saying Air France has gone on strike.

And *then*…

We were taken to a resort hotel. "Be ready to leave tomorrow at two p.m." I had a good room with air-conditioning. Slept well. The gift shop has sunscreen and a filmy cover-up so I can join the bathers on the fine sandy beach in a cozy cove. The water is warm, so pleasant. Had lunch with three interesting ladies. One spoke English! This interlude was, of course, courtesy of Air France. We quickly found our seats on same plane, same crew. Took off at three thirty p.m.

And *then*…

We landed at Haiti! Now here is a place I never expected to be in my whole life. Even though it was only tarmac and it was dark out I had to get off just to breathe Haitian air. Somebody slipped my hand into his. I turned to see a large black man nicely uniformed. He simply led me inside to the ladies'. He was there when I came out and he led me back to the plane. No English. On to Miami. It was close to midnight when I gave up looking for my suitcase. My feet hurt. I found a wheelchair, grabbed a cab for the nearest hotel.

George and I had planned to visit my friend Margery in Fort Myers. I went alone. We had a lovely visit. Went out to dinner twice with impeccably dressed ladies. Me in my bathing slippers.

Flew back to Miami for the flight to Denver, thence to Sheridan. I checked my backpack and settled in for the journey. I will be home this afternoon. Having lived in Denver for three and a half years I knew DIA pretty well. After check-in I marched right down to the end of B Concourse, knowing I had to walk down some stairs then a long ways to the gate. But *nothing* indicated Great Lakes Airlines. I did the stint twice. My feet hurt. A wheelchair took me to Special Services. The kind lady there said my flight had just taken off, the last for the day. It seems that A Concourse opened up a new section for the smaller planes.

And *then*…

Home at last. George met me. He had picked up my suitcase in Miami with no trouble at all.

Know what? I had a ball.

Mary Ralston Hayden Burgess

Daughter of Joseph Ralston Hayden and
Elizabeth "Betty" Olivia Hall Hayden.
Paternal granddaughter of Professor Phillip Cady Hayden
And Mary Neely Ralston Hayden.
Paternal great-granddaughter of Joel B. Hayden and
Fannie J. Van Brocklin Hayden
and Dr. and Mrs. J. N. Ralston.
Maternal granddaughter of Louis Phillips Hall and Elizabeth Douglas Hall.
Maternal great-granddaughter of Olivia Bigelow Hall and Israel Hall.
Sister of Ralston Hayden and Elizabeth Hayden Pearson.
Wife of Henry Amos Burgess.
Mother of Sheridan Samuel Burgess, Mary Helen Burgess Mooney,
Tyler Elizabeth Burgess, Heather Hayden Burgess Plank,
Sarah Louise Burgess, and James Henry Burgess.

Acknowledgements

I am indebted to Val Burgess, Monna Monk, Joan Hellmund and Peggy Slater for putting the hodge-podge together, each encouraging me to dig a little deeper or to pull back; to Molly Mooney for reading the manuscript; to George Ewan for helpful casual remarks; to Kate Swarthout, Marian Adam, and Toni Roberts. To Dana Butler for the title, and to my last editor, my grandson Damon Cole.

Printed in the United States
34987LVS00003B/37-57

9 781418 475734